Right From the Start:

Insights Into Building and Remodeling Your Custom Home

Right From the Start:

Insights Into Building and Remodeling Your Custom Home

Bob Michels

with Dave Konkol

**RIGHT FROM THE START: INSIGHTS INTO BUILDING
AND REMODELING YOUR CUSTOM HOME**
Copyright © 2013 Builders Publishing Group
Published by Builders Publishing Group, LLC
500 N. Maitland Avenue #313, Maitland, FL 32751

General Editor: Todd Chobotar
Production Editor: Katherine Johnson
Project Coordinator: Katherine Johnson
Book Design: Bruce Vogel, The Herman Lewis Design Syndicate

This book is a work of advice and opinion. Neither the authors nor the publisher is responsible for actions based on the content of this book. It is not the purpose of this book to include all information about building a house. The book should be used as a general guide and not as a totality of information on the subject. In addition, materials, techniques and codes are continuously changing so please understand what is printed here may not be the most current information available.

This book contains numerous case histories and client stories. In order to preserve the privacy of the people involved, the authors have disguised their names, appearances, and aspects of their personal stories so that they are not identifiable. Stories may also include composite characters.

ISBN-13: 978-0-9895114-0-8 (Hard Cover)
ISBN-13: 978-0-9895114-1-5 (Soft Cover)

Printed in the United States of America

9 8 7 6 5 4 3 2 1

First Edition

Contents

—⚜—

Dedication

This book is dedicated to my late father, James P. Michels, and uncle Victor N. Michels. They taught me about building, how to treat people well and most importantly, what really matters in life.

Bob Michels

An Important Note
From the Authors

This book is the result of a collaboration between two award-winning custom homebuilders who share common values and ideals. Fellow custom builder Dave Konkol allowed me to modify and rewrite this book to reflect the way that I do business here in suburban St. Paul and Minneapolis, Minnesota. I wanted to write a book that focused on my clients' needs and the issues specific to our area. Some of the stories included are from my personal experiences and advice working with my clients, many of whom have become lifelong friends.

Please note: Although there are two co-authors on the book they have chosen to write in the first person singular (I, me, my, etc.), as if only one person were speaking. This makes both the writing and reading much easier. So, although stories, illustrations, or examples may come from either author, they have been written as if coming from "one voice."

Also note: In order to achieve an easy flow of language, this book has been written using the singular pronoun "he" when referring to a builder. The authors realize there are many wonderful builders who are women, but have chosen to avoid the awkward use of "he/she" and have chosen instead to use the traditional masculine pronoun when referring to a builder. No offense is intended in this regard; the decision was made merely to achieve simplicity and flow of language.

Lastly, though I am a custom home builder, I also have extensive experience as a remodeler of existing homes. Because building and remodeling are similar processes, the book will use the term "builder" in all situations for the ease of readership.

Before You Begin

—⚜—

My father would take me to work when I was a kid. I set to work leveling off boards with the carpenters, hammering in nails with the roofers, sweeping nearly completed houses, and other odd jobs. Even though I was just an extra set of teenage hands, I became an essential part of the project in that moment.

As I got older, my responsibilities in the project became more involved. My father and uncle would bring me into the office to learn the finer points of running a business that was successful in their books, in the community, and in their product. When I finally took over the company in 1981, I was the boss of a company that already enjoyed a great reputation in the community and steeped in three generations of hard work. Today, my own son, Andy, works alongside me.

I have learned many different ways of building and selling a home throughout my career – the art of scheduling, cost control and project management – but I keep coming back to the same principle: *nothing should be assumed and every client is unique*. One size does not fit all in a custom home or remodel. I relish the challenge of making each customer's needs and dreams fit into an attractive and durable home they can enjoy for years to come. With every customer, I like to explore their vision and make purposeful decisions to bring to life a home where they can live, grow, and share their days with family and friends. To me, this is the way to build a custom home.

I believe the true role of a custom homebuilder and remodeler is to make an idea into a home by building relationships, working with the right people, and drawing on my four generations of professional experience. My clients often tell me they feel that their home is truly their own because I cared enough to ask the questions that they didn't even know to ask. My unwavering dedication to my clients, and my commitment to offering an extraordinary level of personal service to only a handful of clients at a time, sets me apart from other builders in the area. I want to build a home that pulls at your heartstrings, that gives you a place to create memories with your children, family, and friends.

Making the decision to build your dream home or remodel your space is both a very personal decision and a very rewarding adventure. If you are lacking the right information, your wishes may not be fulfilled and the project may result in unforeseen problems, delays, and stress. I want this book to serve as your guide and an essential resource. The information contained in this book, based on highlights from my 40-plus years of experience, will help you make more informed choices and experience less stress and greater confidence throughout the entire process.

Everything you need to know about remodeling or building a custom home is in your hands. Are you ready to get started? Let's do this together.

Bob Michels

PART I

BEFORE
YOU BUILD

Should I Build, or Should I Buy an Existing Home?

—⚜—

6 6To build or to buy." That's the primary question to answer before building or remodeling a home. To help you decide, ask yourself these ten important questions. Be very honest. Answer each one carefully. Keep in mind that there are no right or wrong answers. You're simply trying to determine the best course of action at this point in your life.

Questions to consider.   Yes or No

—⚜—————————————————————————————

1. Do I have a hard time making decisions? ☐ ☐

2. Once I make decisions, do I struggle with wanting to change them? ☐ ☐

3. Am I a perfectionist? ☐ ☐

4. Is my schedule so busy it's difficult to find time to do the things I enjoy? ☐ ☐

5. Does uncertainty and lack of control add stress to my life? ☐ ☐

6. Am I regularly disappointed by interactions with other people? ☐ ☐

7. Do I handle conflict by looking for the win/win solution? ☐ ☐

8. Do I have some available time in my life for the next two to three years? ☐ ☐

9. Am I realistic enough to recognize that things aren't always perfect? ☐ ☐

10. Is our family life stable enough to handle the additional activity? ☐ ☐

—————————————————————————————⚜—

If you answered "no" to the first six questions and "yes" to the last four, you're ready to build! If not, you may want to consider waiting on the building process. If your answers were different on more than three or four questions, I suggest you buy a house that is already built.

In a consumer-driven economy, many families have been stretched and stressed because the timing wasn't right or they weren't the right profile of person to be building a custom home. They would've been better off buying an existing home than going through a process that wasn't suited for their life stage, temperament, or timing.

Let's look at an example of a couple that wasn't ready for the custom homebuilding process: In some ways, Brad and Melinda seemed to be ideal candidates to custom design and build a new home. However, it soon became apparent they had difficulty making decisions (see question #1). In addition, Brad was consumed by the demands of his business since he had just launched his own company three years before (see questions #4 and #8).

Brad and Melinda were habitually late for their appointments. In addition to the pressing demands of business, once they made a decision, they would always second guess and revisit previous decisions (see question #2). It became apparent that this lovely couple did not have the time at this point in their lives to spend custom designing and building a home. A quick look at the 10 questions above clearly indicated it wasn't an ideal time for Brad and Melinda to build a new home.

BOTTOM LINE

Carefully consider the decision to build or to buy before beginning the design/build process.

Which Comes First:
The Builder or the Designer?

—eᴓ—

Just like the proverbial "chicken and egg" question, "Which comes first?" is a question that confuses some people, but must be answered before you start the custom, homebuilding process. While the answer may seem obvious, it's important to know the right answer in order to avoid problems from the beginning. The designer comes before the builder, right?

Wrong! Read on...

Sometimes people get the cart before the horse and in all the excitement, they get ahead of themselves. Jay and Betsy thought they had done it all right. They had a roll of plans tucked under their arms, a sparkle in their eyes, and a skip in their steps because they knew they had something very special—they had the plans to their dream home.

During the last several months, Jay and Betsy had spent countless hours dreaming about their new home and holding meetings with their designer. They went through revision after revision pouring over the plans until late in the evenings. The couple worked tirelessly to make every room just right—put the baby's room here, move the daughter's room there, make that closet just a bit wider, add two feet to the kitchen—giving instruction upon instruction to their designer about each room.

Their dream home included the newest ideas from *This Old House*, the latest trends in low voltage lighting, and cutting-edge insulation that could lower energy bills by up to 90 percent. It had a cabana like the one they saw while vacationing in Acapulco, layers upon layers of moldings, extra tall ceilings, an additional bay in the garage, a steeper roof that was changed—not twice, but three times—because their friends told them it looked too shallow.

Jay and Betsy were now ready to find a builder. They were so excited! Betsy was bubbling over with her plans—holiday decorations, birthday parties, and dinners with all the aunts, uncles, cousins, and grandma. They had their finished plans and they were now ready to build. They could see it; they could taste it; they could hear the sounds of laughter around the table.

And then the moment of truth arrived.

They were ready to talk to a builder and get him started on their new house. But here was the problem: the actual cost to build this house—the house they had labored over for so many hours, over so many months—ended up costing 75 percent more to build than they expected.

How did this happen? Well—they asked the designer and he gave them his estimate of what it would cost. That's what they based their plans on. *The designer's estimate*.

And that is the problem. The designer and architect are not trained in doing cost estimates. This news was so devastating to them that Jay and Betsy just rolled up their plans, walked out the door, and… sold their lot.

Their dreams had been shattered and they were crushed. After all their initial efforts, they couldn't gather the energy to start the process all over again. But it could have been different. If only this enthusiastic couple had known the importance of which comes first: the builder, not the designer.

If you're in this predicament and you're unwilling to sell your lot, turn the page and discover what happens next by reading Jim and Linda's story.

BOTTOM LINE

Meet with your builder and discuss your budget before you meet with a designer.

Forcing a Round Peg Into a Square Hole
Finding a Competent Builder

—⚬ᴗ⚬—

Jim and Linda were the kind of people who refuse to give up. Sometimes persistence is a good thing, but there are times when pushing too hard is unwise. This couple, for instance, were unwilling to listen to sound, professional advice. They forced their opinions and ideas on a builder— and it was like forcing a round peg into a square hole. It just didn't work. Even when they realized they had received inaccurate advice from their designer about their homebuilding costs, they wouldn't give up their dream.

So they began to shop in earnest for a builder who would build their home for the price they were told. Would Jim and Linda find a satisfactory and skilled homebuilder?

Maybe. But the builder they seemed to want—one who would be the answer to all their problems—would have been either a builder who was desperate for work or one who didn't know how to price a home.

Finding a competent builder can be challenging, but when you know what to look for, you'll get an accurate estimate and good advice. Many builders won't (or don't know how to) price a home while it's still in the concept stage. If most *builders* can't do this, it certainly makes sense that most *designers* can't either. After all, designers are trained and skilled in *designing* and creating what they are asked to create. Homeowners who don't have a good handle on pricing will tell the designer what they want and the designer will only do what he was retained to do. I'm not blaming designers for not knowing about estimating accurate costs; it's not their area of expertise.

After dozens of exhausting interviews with many builders, Jim and Linda got their homebuilding costs down to a price that was only 20 or 30 percent less than the initial estimate—still well over their budget. But they didn't want to give up their dream; they were willing to do anything to bring their dream to fruition.

At this point, Jim and Linda had some choices to make. Instead of cutting their losses and stopping the spending, they continued to pour more and more money into a project that wasn't suitable.

There are plenty of potential homeowners who receive bad advice from a builder and find out one or two years later that their building project is a disaster. Sometimes they begin frantically calling reputable builders in the middle of a project, pleading for help because they finally realize they have relied on poor advice and ended up involved in a lawsuit with their builder.

Please don't do this to yourself. Save yourself and your family the agony of lost time, lost dreams, or lawsuits. Life is too short. It's not worth it.

Get good advice from a competent builder. Interview several first to determine the right one for you and your custom home project. A competent builder will explain the homebuilding process and all the steps along the way. He can guide you through the entire process so you feel confident and secure in your purchase decisions. His firm will have an excellent reputation and be up-to-date on building codes, land, and procedures. Check out the company's references and previous projects completed.

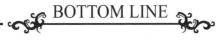

BOTTOM LINE

Make sure you get good advice from a competent builder.

Do I Have to Like My Builder?

———✦———

S o now you've selected a competent builder. But you may ask, "Do I have to like the guy? If he has a good reputation as a builder, does it really matter if I like him?"

Yes, it matters. Don't sign a contract with a builder you don't like, trust, or respect. If you do, you could be headed for trouble.

Why? Because this is a long-term relationship and a long-term relationship with someone you don't like, trust, or respect can be challenging, frustrating, and more than disappointing. The planning stages of custom building a new home can take anywhere from months to years. Actual construction may range from six months to 24 months or longer, depending on the size and scope of your home. Add to that a one- or two-year limited warranty time period, and Minnesota's ten-year structural warranty period, as well as the fact that you may need additional information from your builder for many years to come regarding warranty information, vendor and subcontractor contacts, and other nuances.

In this business, it's not uncommon to lose some contracts to other builders, and it usually boils down to *perceived* costs. A prospective homeowner may initially think our pricing is higher than our competitor, but most often that's because we didn't have the opportunity to thoroughly compare the two proposals. Comparing apples to oranges is confusing, but an analysis of two proposals can be revealing.

We like to ask our homeowners why they chose us to build their home. Often the answer is trust. When challenges arise in your project and you call to ask questions, it's important to know that you'll get a straight and honest answer.

Do you respect your builder's values? You don't have to socialize together, but sometimes people choose a builder they actually dislike. Maybe the husband likes the builder or his price, but his wife doesn't care for his style, approach, or manners. Ask yourself this question: Is there a reason you're uncomfortable with this person? If so, why in the world would you trust him to build your single most important investment? If you or your spouse sense that a potential builder operates from a less-than-honest value system, why would you trust him to operate his business with honest values?

During the construction process there will be times when your builder will be making some judgment calls. Many of these will be unknown to you, and that's just part of the business. When it comes to your home, you'll want to know that your builder will be making choices as if it's his own home, *as if his own family's safety depended on the choices he makes*. Not just what will pass code inspections. No shortcuts for a quick profit.

Are values important? You bet they are!

BOTTOM LINE

Don't sign a contract with someone you don't like, trust, or respect.

Pick Three Out of Four
Quality, Speed, Service, Price

—ℯℽↄ—

Jim and Susan had six—count 'em, six—separate flooring companies at their home in a three week period providing estimates to sand and refinish their hardwood floors. About a month later, an unusual sound came from Jim and Susan's house, loud enough that everyone in the neighborhood heard it. There was an explosion of screaming and yelling that continued for several minutes. A hardwood flooring van was parked out front; can you guess what happened? The couple expected a beautiful, high-quality floor, but what they got was what they paid for. They were not happy.

Jim and Susan had selected their hardwood flooring contractor based strictly on price, but somehow they expected they would receive quality, speed, service, *and* the best price. Sure, they probably got the lowest price, but with it came a lot of heartache because they expected more and got a lot less.

It's no different than selecting a builder for your custom home. You need to determine what you value and decide what's most important: quality, speed, service, or price. Of course, you want all four components, but most often you will need to find a builder who can provide three out of four. That's reality. Is it reasonable to expect that you'll get a builder who will give you the lowest price with great quality, great service, and a timely finish?

Let's consider the merits of each:

1. Quality: A good company prides itself on providing a quality product, especially in the custom home market. They encourage prospective homeowners to look closely at the work they've done for other homeowners and affirm they would be pleased with the excellent workmanship the company provides. Comfort with quality, luxury with outstanding craftsmanship.

2. Speed: An on-time finish is important, but there may be times, especially in a busy market, when a builder misses some deadlines. If that happens, you want your builder to proactively communicate with you and, if possible, find a way to make up the time and get it done quickly.

3. Service: A builder with exceptional customer care will provide good communication and attend to the homeowner's needs before, during, and after their home is completed.

4. Price: The best companies aren't usually the cheapest, but consider this: they're probably not the most expensive either. Great companies deliver good value. An honest builder charges at or below market value for the level of service and quality product they provide. Very seldom is the cheapest price the best choice for a homebuilder.

Don't make the mistake of thinking you can have all four qualities in one builder. A Lexus or a Mercedes is priced differently than a Buick. If you pay Buick pricing (like Jim and Susan) and still expect a Lexus or Mercedes level of performance, you are setting yourself up for disappointment, conflict, and sometimes even a lawsuit.

Know what's important to you and adjust your expectations. If cost is your most important value, then choose the contract with the lowest price. However, if you value quality, be sure you look for excellent workmanship. You can get the results you want in a quality, custom home; just be sure to select your builder based on what you truly value.

BOTTOM LINE

Realistically expect to get three out of four components from your homebuilder. Decide what is important to you.

Where Should I Spend My Money?
If You're Going to Err, Do It Here

Building or totally renovating a home is probably one of the biggest investments you'll ever make, so you'll want to know where to put your money to get the most value for your investment.

Here are seven areas to consider:

1. Location: You've heard the adage "location, location, location." This is where to spend your money. You could build a home with a great design with great features and finishes, but if you build or remodel it in the wrong location or on the wrong lot, you could be in real trouble. Consider purchasing the most expensive lot you can afford. Historically, waterfront property experiences stronger growth in value than non-waterfront property. If you like water and can afford it, build on waterfront. Your long-term investment is more likely to be sound.

2. Design Services: You can add enormous value to your home by investing in the services of a competent designer and an interior design team. Not only will you enjoy the splendor of a fabulous home, you will find a greater return on the money you spend for these services at the time of resale. Great design is the first money you will spend on your project; it is also the most important.

3. Kitchen: Most buyers don't complain about a kitchen being too large, too much counter space, or too many cabinets. Spend money on the kitchen. We'll talk more about this topic later.

4. Family Room: Oversize, don't undersize, your family room. Families tend to gather and spend most of their time in the family room. If you were to oversize any room, make this room a little larger (rather than smaller) than you think you need.

5. Master Bath: This room is the owner's retreat, a place to relax and unwind. Upgrade your master bath's size and finishes. When you sell your home, this will be an important feature and provide a good investment return.

6. Room Size: Make sure your rooms are large enough to meet your needs. It's very expensive to come back after your home is finished and add twelve or eighteen inches to a room because you've just realized it's too small. If you're on a limited budget, it's better to hold off on some of the finishes than cut down the size of your rooms. You can add finishes later, and the cost may only be slightly higher than if you installed them during the initial construction process.

7. Closets: Never underestimate the value of roomy walk-in closets, linen closets, and laundry rooms.

BOTTOM LINE

Invest your money in the seven places that matter most and you will experience great value for years to come.

What's So Important About the Kitchen Anyway?

—⟨ৡৡ⟩—

When a couple buys, builds, or remodels a home, they always seem to pay a lot of attention to the kitchen. With most couples, there's usually one person who loves to cook; most often it's the woman. But for everyone, male or female, young or old, the kitchen is one of the most important rooms in the house. The kitchen is often the hub of the home, the center of activity. Someone spends time preparing food, creating something fun, or trying a new recipe in it. People tend to gather where there's food.

So don't miss this: kitchens are important!

Men sometimes underestimate the importance of this room. We love our garages, grills, decks, and patios. But the kitchen? We can completely miss its importance.

It's important to remember when you are designing a home to consider the resale value and design accordingly. A well-designed and functional kitchen not only makes the cook happy, it also ensures a greater resale value.

A person who loves to cook or create culinary masterpieces for family and friends absolutely needs a spacious and well-appointed kitchen. On the other hand, if a cook wants to spend as little time as possible in the kitchen, then your design and layout can be simpler. Kathy doesn't spend much time in her kitchen, but she likes the spacious layout so she and her husband can be there together. Kathy says the chopping and stirring are more enjoyable with her husband there. Additionally, he likes the organization of a well-planned room.

When selecting kitchen cabinets, look for quality. This is not the place to be overly consumed with trying to save money. Well-made cabinets will provide lasting pleasure and functionality for decades. Drawers (as opposed to cabinets with doors) are more useful and efficient even compared to cabinets with pullout drawers. In addition, choose hard surface, durable, and high quality countertops. There are a variety of colors and selections available. Granite is an ideal counter surface for the most important room in the house. Be sure to consider Cambria when looking at the upper price levels of solid surface counter tops. The latest fashion trends and colors are available in this top of the line product.

What about appliances? Don't skimp here, either. You don't have to purchase the absolute top of the line, but good quality appliances help sell homes. Today it's becoming very popular to have two dishwashers. Often the cost of an additional dishwasher is only slightly more than the cost of the additional cabinetry it replaces.

In order to make the most important room in your house spectacular, consider adding some of these other features: warming drawers, double ovens, convection microwaves, pot fillers, espresso and coffee bars, hidden pantries, elevated dishwashers for easy access, vegetable sinks in the island (in addition to the main sink), instant hot water dispensers, and purified water faucets. In my experience, our customers have found a large island to be the highlight of their kitchen. A large, beautiful island with ample space around it tends to be the centerpiece of many family and informal gatherings.

When you design your home, be sure the kitchen is given special consideration and that its relationship to other rooms, functions, and features are the best you can provide. It will make a difference for years to come.

BOTTOM LINE

Don't treat your kitchen like any other room in your home. This is one room that deserves special treatment.

Needs Vs. Wants
How to Use The Design Outline to Prioritize Yours

— славо—

One of the best things a homeowner can do is to thoughtfully consider the difference between needs and wants. It's more difficult than it sounds. For example, something that is considered a *need* to one family member may not be viewed that way by another. Sorting between needs and wants can sometimes be contentious. Take Tim and Sherri for instance. They debated for 45 minutes on whether or not they wanted a formal living room. Sherri, who was raised in a home that frequently entertained guests, considered it a need. Tim, whose idea of entertaining guests was to take them to the game room, did not consider it a need. In fact, Tim felt a formal living room would be largely wasted space.

Discussions like these are far from unusual when building a custom home. They are normal—even essential. I encourage couples and families to have these discussions as soon as possible so that decisions can be made before a lot of design work is done. But how can you have those discussions and make them productive and even enjoyable? By using a simple tool called The Design Outline.

The Design Outline is an excellent tool to help you define your needs and wants in the home building process. This exercise takes less than 30 minutes to complete, but it can save you countless hours and thousands of dollars.

Here's how it works:

➻ You and your spouse, independently of each other, each take a blank sheet of paper and write down all of your dreams, wants, and needs for your new home, in no particular order.

➻ Then rank your items in order of importance, starting with #1, #2, #3, etc. It's not as important to agonize over whether item two goes before item three, or three before two; sometimes wants or needs can be equally important to you. What's important here is that #3 and #28 are not reversed. Know what you want.

➻ Once you and your spouse have independently ranked your items, the two of you meet together to share and compare your lists. Then create one combined list ranking your needs and wants in order. This will become your master list.

The combined needs/wants list will save time, energy, and money when you meet with your builder to determine the cost of your new dream home. At some point, your desired budget will need to line up with your desired wants.

Your builder can review this combined list and your budget and let you know what items your budget can afford. If you have items that are not included in the budget, your builder can estimate a cost so you can make an informed decision on whether or not you want to increase your original budget.

The Design Outline can be a tremendously effective tool to help you determine costs long before you spend money on design or construction of your new custom home. You can use The Design Outline with any builder, anywhere in the country. When you begin the process by using the outline, you'll be way ahead of the game.

THE DESIGN OUTLINE™

Name:					
Address of Property:					
Lot#:	Cost of Lot:		Value of Lot Today:		
Estimated budget for home excluding lot and financing costs:					
Number of Bedrooms:		Number of Bathrooms:			
Approx. number of square feet under air:					
Number of Stories:	One	Two	Bays in Garage	Two	Three	Four

COMBINED LIST OF PRIORITIES

1.		11.	
2.		12.	
3.		13.	
4.		14.	
5.		15.	
6.		16.	
7.		17.	
8.		18.	
9.		19.	
10.		20.	

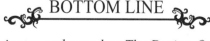

BOTTOM LINE

Take thirty minutes and complete The Design Outline. It's fun and can save you countless hours and thousands of dollars.

Should I Use a Fixed-Price or Cost-Plus Contract?
Part 1–Fixed-Price

—⟳⟳—

A fixed-price contract is one in which the plans, specifications, and all of the materials and finishes are fully determined (fixed) before you start construction on your new home. A cost-plus contract takes all the costs of the home and adds either a percentage of costs or a flat fee for the builder's overhead and management fee.

Either a fixed-price or a cost-plus contract can be used successfully in building a custom home. It depends on what you're most comfortable with. The builder's costs are the same whether he uses a fixed-price or cost-plus contract. However, the price you'll pay will differ because of the risk associated with each type of contract. I always provide a detailed spreadsheet for my customers so that they may review my costs, overhead, and profit. This not only helps my customers better understand their investment, but it also builds trust in our relationship.

Let's start by looking at a fixed-price contract.

The advantage of a fixed-price contract is that the price you pay for your home will be predetermined (fixed) whether or not the price of material and labor goes up or down. The builder assumes full responsibility for all risks associated with the cost of your new home. The downside is that you'll pay more for your builder taking on this risk.

On a fixed-price contract, the builder assumes responsibility for all risks associated with the fluctuation in costs. Of course, costs are always changing. From the time you sign your contract to the completion of the work, the actual costs will change. Sometimes up, sometimes down. If labor and material go down from the time you sign the contract until the job is complete, the builder benefits. If the cost of labor and material go up during the construction period, the builder absorbs the loss. Another factor in pricing a home with a fixed-price contract involves the "fright factor." Will the homeowners change their demeanor once construction begins? No one has ever built a perfect home without some sort of scratch or blemish on it. Any builder can walk into any home in America and find something that's wrong. Anyone can take a magnifying glass and find scratches on any window on any newly built home in America.

Therefore, builders need to charge clients for "fright." If the builder gets to the final walk-through with a homeowner who takes out a magnifying glass and searches every square inch of every window pane in the house, finds a scratch, and wants every scratched window replaced—at the builder's expense—the builder had better have "fright" included in his initial calculations. With a fixed-price contract, the cost of repairing or replacing any and every item that has even a tiny imperfection is all the builder's responsibility.

Generally, people with a fixed-price contract are more inclined to expect imperfect minor items to be replaced because it doesn't cost them extra. To be clear, we're not talking about shoddy workmanship. We're talking about the gray areas of requests that are unreasonable, based on industry standards.

In general, people who do well with a fixed-price contract are people who are not willing to risk price fluctuations. They are more comfortable knowing their exact cost and are willing to pay a small premium for this comfort.

In the next chapter, we will cover the cost-plus contract.

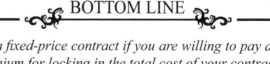

BOTTOM LINE

Choose a fixed-price contract if you are willing to pay a small premium for locking in the total cost of your contract.

Should I Use a Fixed-Price or Cost-Plus Contract?
Part 2–Cost Plus

—ᴄᴗᴣᴏ—

A cost-plus contract differs from a fixed-price contract in that it takes the actual cost of building or remodeling the home and adds a fee for the builder's overhead and management. This fee can be either a lump sum (flat fee) or a percentage of total costs. Of course, neither you nor your builder will know the exact bottom line for the building costs until the final accounting is completed shortly after closing. A good builder will give you an accurate cost estimate, but it's exactly that—an estimate—until the final accounting. With a cost-plus contract, you'll pay the actual costs for all labor and material, plus the builder's fee.

A cost-plus contract can be advantageous when building larger, custom homes with finish levels and other things changing during the process. With the cost-plus basis, the homeowners know their actual costs on an ongoing basis. They can then determine where they will appropriate their funds early in the construction process and receive a full accounting disclosure of all costs.

It doesn't mean the builder builds with less care or quality; it just puts the homeowner and the builder on the same team. A cost-plus contract provides the synergy of identifying problems and determining win/win solutions that are in the best interests of the homeowner.

If you trust that your builder is competent and is working on your behalf, and if you are comfortable not knowing your exact total costs until the end of the project, then a cost-plus contract may be best for you. Your final cost will depend on the choices you make. Your builder will charge a smaller management fee on a cost-plus basis because he assumes less risk.

Both fixed-price and cost-plus contracts are successfully used in building new custom homes. You can decide which one works best for you.

BOTTOM LINE

Choose a cost-plus contract if you are comfortable knowing your end cost will be determined by the choices you make and you know you have a trustworthy builder.

Don't Even Begin Designing Your Home
Until You've Done This!

—❧—

There is an ancient proverb that says, *"Suppose one of you wants to build a tower. Will he not first sit down and estimate the cost to see if he has enough money to complete it?"* I suppose it's because I'm a builder, but I can relate to this bit of wisdom. It's a rhetorical question, of course. Who wouldn't first estimate the cost?

In reality, it sometimes amazes me to meet with people who are ready to build or remodel their home but have no idea what they want or how much they can spend. Stop right here! It's crucial, before beginning the design/build process, to determine what you can afford.

People who need financing assistance should talk to an experienced professional mortgage lender who can help determine what they can comfortably afford. This process will take into account your income, expenses, credit, assets, interest rate, taxes, insurance, maintenance, and utilities.

Sadly, people who begin the design process without first counting the cost often design to their dreams, only to find out later they have far exceeded what they can afford. They end up mad, sad, or extremely frustrated. Instead, we first want our homeowners to realistically determine what they can afford; then we work hard to design a quality, custom home, a complete package that's 5 to 10 percent below their target number. We know from experience that changes may occur during the building process. For instance, a homeowner may upgrade the finishes as the construction process unfolds, or other variables may arise that would add to the cost of their home. If we start with a number that is below their budget, we can end up at the desired budget.

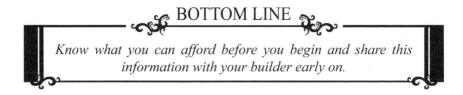

BOTTOM LINE

Know what you can afford before you begin and share this information with your builder early on.

Buy a Plan or Custom Design?
Read This Before You Decide

—❧—

Should you buy a ready-made plan for constructing your new home? It depends.

If you have a large flat lot that doesn't have restrictive setbacks, then finding and buying a ready-made plan may work well for you. It's important to know that most plans you find in a plan book are designed for specific lot sizes and regular shaped lots. If your lot is long and narrow and the plan is designed for a lot that's narrow and long (just the opposite), you could have a problem. Furthermore, lake lots and the sites of tear-downs are usually very challenging. A local builder who is familiar with setbacks, easements, and local ordinances will be an asset in evaluating a proposed building site.

Sometimes people will use the "cut-and-paste" method. A couple will take a plan from a plan book and "cut-and-paste" it to make it fit their lot. Be careful with this method. Judy was a woman whose cut-and-paste plan didn't work out the way she'd planned; it required you to walk through one bedroom to get to another bedroom.

If you can find a plan that fits on your lot with little or no changes, it may be a good option for you. However, very few people are completely happy with a design they find in a plan book without making minor to major modifications.

If you are thinking of buying a ready-made plan and just shrinking it, it almost certainly will *not* work.

Most good, custom-home builders have successfully built homes from ready-made plans. Typically they purchase the rights for the plan, make any needed modifications, and proceed to build the house.

Be aware that ready-made plans are copyrighted. Your builder can purchase the rights for the plan, but be sure this step is not overlooked. You can get in real trouble down the road if you shortcut this step.

For people who don't choose a standard plan, some builders offer a complete design/build package. Usually this process starts by evaluating the shape of the lot; it's important to take into account its positive and negative features. The builder then takes the homeowner's completed list of their prioritized needs and wants and begins the design process. At your initial meeting with the builder, it's an important step to review the design and to ensure the designer and homeowner have a complete and thorough understanding of needs, wants, and budget. Once the builder has clearly identified your objectives, he can work with the designer to create a unique, quality, custom home—the home of your dreams.

As a builder, I've found that it doesn't necessarily cost any more (and often we've discovered cost savings) by first focusing on and designing what our homeowners most *need* while also taking into account what they want. In doing so, we've found great success because the process allows us to optimize the conditions of the specific and unique lot instead of having to work from an existing design by enlarging or shrinking areas in the home.

With clear objectives and a good plan, you can focus your energy and resources on your unique needs for your new home.

BOTTOM LINE

If you can find a ready-made plan that requires few or no changes and you just love it, then you may want to consider purchasing a buyer-ready plan. If not, don't make the mistake of cutting and pasting.

Surprises That Could Inflate Your Custom Home Cost

—ↄﻭↄ﮺—

E arly in the design process, your builder should work with you to create an estimated line-item budget for your home. Each item (landscaping, appliances, flooring, etc.) should be listed separately with a corresponding dollar amount (allowance). The line-item budget should make sense to you, and the numbers should be in line with the general caliber of work you've seen in other homes this builder has completed.

Interestingly, an allowance (or budget) can be your friend or it can be your worst enemy. Good, honest, quality builders may lose jobs to the competition because they establish a realistic allowance that truly reflects the scope of the entire job. Conversely, many builders will establish low allowances that are insufficient to build the home with the quality expected. Be wary of a budget that seems too good to be true. You could be talking to an unscrupulous builder who says whatever he has to say to get your business.

Allowances are established by builders because selections are not always made prior to the commencement of building a new home. If a builder provides an estimate for a new home and purposely or unknowingly lists allowances that are not sufficient for the quality expected, the initial bid can be thousands, if not tens of thousands, less than an honest builder's proposal.

The last thing anyone needs is to be in the middle of construction with insufficient allowances to complete the home. A good, quality builder will put a lot of effort into listening to what a homeowner values and then designing a complete home package to meet those needs. He will try to establish budgets (allowances) that allow the homeowners to select items that are in line with the level of quality they want for their home.

One of the biggest challenges for a homeowner and a builder is to identify a sufficient allowance and how all those numbers and allowances play into an overall budget. The major keys to a successful project are to take the desired overall budget, consider the needs and wants of the homeowner, and create and execute a home that the homeowner will be happy with for years to come.

After listening to the needs of the homeowners, a builder will establish allowances that are appropriate for that home. After that, you should do some shopping at selected vendors before you sign a contract. This will allow you to get a sense as to whether the allowances are sufficient. If the allowances are not sufficient, you either have to raise the overall budget or reduce allowances or features in other parts of the home. It's important to do this *before* construction begins. If determining allowances happens *after* construction begins, it leaves room for misunderstanding and frustration.

BOTTOM LINE

Know what your allowances will buy for your new home before you sign a contract.

Design Your New Home with Resale in Mind

14

—⁂—

W ho thinks about resale value when building or remodeling a home? While it may seem odd for a person who's building to think about selling it, it's important to address what you want and what the market wants even in the initial planning stages. If you're not careful, you may design your dream home and find that no one else will buy it later!

Most people who build or remodel custom homes are financially sound. For the most part, they are able to build beautiful, quality homes because they've been making good financial decisions for many years. As you go through your design process, be certain you get wise counsel from your builder, designer, and possibly a real estate salesperson to be sure you're not building a home that only your family will like. Balance your wants and needs for the home of your dreams with potential market appeal for future resale.

You are probably not building your dream home as a spec home (a home without an end buyer before construction begins, generally built with an intended profit), so be careful not to include design features that are not what the broad market is asking for. An experienced builder will guide you through the design process and help protect your investment. Once you have the facts, it's your responsibility to make your own design decisions. If you proceed to design and build a home that only appeals to a very narrow market, then at least you are aware of that (and the consequences) in the early stages of the design process.

Sometimes homes linger on the market for a long time because a homeowner made design decisions without taking into account the long-term resale effects.

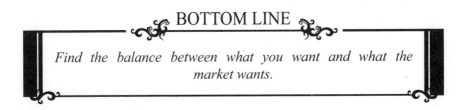

⁂ BOTTOM LINE ⁂

Find the balance between what you want and what the market wants.

You're Going to Live Here HOW Long?

—✺—

If you ask someone who is ready to build or remodel a home, they will often tell you that "This is the last home I will ever live in. They will have to bury me in the backyard."

Recent surveys show that most people live in their home an average of five years, and you're probably not much different. You may be thinking, *but this really is going to be my last home.* And if it is, that's great. But you may want to consider the reality of averages.

Mary took more than a year to design her new home for her family, only to discover she was way over budget. She also realized that by the time she completed her home construction, all but one of her five children would be away at college, and she had designed bedrooms for each of them! Reality finally dawned on her—within a few short years, she and her husband would be empty-nesters. Designing her home for a family of seven thinking this would be her home for the rest of her life didn't fit the reality of Mary's imminent transition to a home for two.

When designing your custom home, first design for your immediate needs. Second, take into account what market conditions will allow for your particular home design. Third, give strong consideration to how long you may live in your home. Mary may shift gears and design a home that's perfect for her family's needs for the next five to seven years, with a plan to downsize at that time. With this more realistic outlook, she may give additional consideration to the resale value of her choices.

Don't make the mistake of over-designing a home that may become obsolete for your family within a short period of time.

BOTTOM LINE

Be realistic about your short-term and long-term needs and how long you will live in your home, and design accordingly.

Should I Hire an Attorney?

Some people just feel better if their attorney reviews the construction contract, and that's okay. If you do this, be sure you hire someone who knows the real estate and construction business and will complement the process.

In my own business, my customers and their attorneys recognize that our contract is neutral and does not favor one party over the other.

If you do not feel comfortable with the contract offered by your builder, you may want to consult your attorney.

If you hire an attorney, be sure to hire someone with construction and real estate experience, not a general practice attorney who counsels on personal business, family trusts, estates, etc.

BOTTOM LINE

Hire an attorney to review your contract if it makes you feel better. Just be certain to hire one who helps you and not hinders you.

How Much Do You Charge
Per Square Foot?

—cz∞—

Building or remodeling a custom home is a bit like buying a new car, right? Not exactly.

If you asked a car dealer how much he charges *per pound*, you'd get some very strange looks. Of course, there is some correlation between the cost of the car and its weight, but not significant enough to prompt that question. We all know car dealers don't sell by the pound.

In the same way, I feel perplexed when someone asks me how much I charge *per square foot* to build a home. It's not the right question. There are three factors that contribute to the cost of a home, regardless of where it's built: complexity, level of finish, size and components.

1. Complexity: A home with more features and greater complexity requires more labor, and therefore costs more to build. For example, a rectangular house with four basic corners is less expensive to build than a three-story home with 40 corners, angled walls, and steep roofs, because the latter is more complex and takes more time to complete.

2. Level of Finish: Obviously, vinyl flooring is much less expensive than wood or stone. Formica countertops are less expensive than granite. Twelve-inch baseboards cost more than six-inch baseboards, and a lot of molding is more expensive than no molding at all. The level of finish you choose for your home will have a significant impact on the home's final cost.

3. Size and Components: Size matters in homebuilding costs. A 6,000-square-foot home will cost more than a 2,000-square-foot home. A 2,000-square-foot home would probably include a two-car garage, while a 6,000-square-foot home normally has three or four bays. So not only does the larger home cost more due to the size of the heated and air-conditioned space, but it also takes into account things like garages, number and size of porches, whether the home has a pool, boat dock, circular drive, and other costly components.

It's a good idea to ask a builder what price range per square foot he builds at, in order to know if you're talking with the right builder.

The formula I give to my customers is (quality of products used + level of detail) multiplied by the square footage proposed.

BOTTOM LINE

Don't go to a Chevy dealership if you want to buy a Lexus.

Welcome to Art Class!
Create a Dream Home Notebook

—ঞ৯০—

Now you get to have some fun! While you continue to dream about the possibilities for your custom home, let's create a "Dream Home Notebook." Gather some magazines and tear out pictures of features you really like or want in your home and, just like you did in art class, start collecting them in a notebook. Another great source of design ideas is the website Houzz. It's the online equivalence of clipping décor magazines pages. Respected builders, remodeling firms and designers post pictures of their completed projects online. Most pictures identify the materials and color selections used. This is a great source of "notebook clippings" for you to communicate ideas to your builder and designer. You may also want to take photos of features in other homes you have walked through. Model homes, friends, or neighbors' homes can be great sources of ideas. Write on each picture specifically what it is you like about it. Why did you tear it out? People often begin collecting pictures but months later they can't recall why they tore it out in the first place. Write it down.

Creating your Dream Home Notebook can be an inspiring and enjoyable activity, and it will be very helpful to your builder and design team. As you accumulate more and more pictures, begin to categorize them.

Here are some suggestions for your categories:

౭→ Exterior features

౭→ Kitchen features

౭→ Master bathroom and bedroom

౭→ Common living spaces

౭→ Specialty items such as fireplaces, mantles, trim details, paint colors, etc.

౭→ Colors, textures, styles

❧ Any floor plan that interests you. Write down what interests you about a particular plan. It may be the relationship of rooms, the uniqueness of design, or even a small feature like a hidden pantry or a workstation for mom.

❧ Things you specifically DON'T like

❧ Your written notes

Sometimes it can be difficult to express what you like and don't like in new home features. So the Dream Home Notebook is a helpful resource in the planning process. The saying, *"A picture is worth a thousand words"* also applies to the development of your custom home design. An experienced builder can look at the pictures and listen to the conversation (and often read between the lines) to help you better articulate what you are thinking but are unable to put into words. It's also helpful to write down your expectations. You may want to include stories (good and bad) of what your friends have gone through in their homebuilding experience. Also write down the elements in your home that are important to you. When you finally meet with your builder, you will have a well-organized, thoughtful notebook to share, which will help tremendously in your design and building process.

BOTTOM LINE

Cut out or take pictures for your dream home and organize them in a single place along with your notes on what you really want.

Close Enough to Perfect?
Identifying Expectations

—❧—

A homebuilder's goal is to create a well-built, attractive home that meets the needs of the homeowners. But how close to perfect does the finished product need to be? What about imperfections or flaws? Larry doesn't care about details, while Peter is extremely particular and wants every single blemish erased—*every single one.*

What about you? What are your expectations for what you will and will not accept when your home is finally completed? This is definitely something you and your builder need to discuss.

Here's what I often do: I make an appointment to meet the new prospective homeowner at one of our recently completed homes. I have a very defined plan to walk through this new home together and thoroughly inspect all aspects of the home. We take about one hour of uninterrupted, private time with or without the owner present.

I meet the prospective homeowners at the newly-built home and start the inspection in the foyer. As I point out the features, I ask a very specific question. "If we were standing here a year from today and we were doing the final walk-through on *your* new home, would this meet your expectations?" Usually, my wide-eyed prospective homeowners nod affirmatively. Before I move on to the next room, I take a moment and encourage them to look closely at the finish. I tell them that a paint job can never be perfect; I may find a blemish or two on the walls or in the trim work. Then I ask again, "Would a paint job with these imperfections meet your expectations?" Usually, they say yes. Then I ask them to rub their hands over the trim work to feel for smoothness and any imperfections. I'm actually looking for some imperfections in the paint job because I want to clearly identify their expectations.

After we discuss the paint finish, we move on to trim work. From trim work, we move to drywall. From drywall, we move to flooring, and on and on it goes throughout the house. Then we walk into the living room where the same process takes place. I ask the prospective homeowner the same question, "If this was your living room, aside from the paint colors and selections of materials, would this living room and the quality of the workmanship meet your expectations?"

This process is very important. The last thing you or your builder want is to find yourself a year or 18 months into the building of your new custom home, only to discover that each of you had different expectations. I make it a point during the interview process to be sure we have clear expectations of what is or is not acceptable for the quality of the end product—your custom home. By doing so, both parties can avoid unmet expectations, frustration, anger, or even a lawsuit.

BOTTOM LINE

Schedule a one-hour private showing of a home your builder has recently completed. Tell your builder whether the quality meets your expectations or not.

The Terrible Truth About Building
Beyond Your Means

—cᴏ᷈ꝫ—

Of course, I know I'm not my clients' keeper regarding how they spend their money. But as a professional who values integrity, I believe I have a responsibility to share the cold, hard facts of the large investment they will be making in building a home. Some people begin the design process with a realistic budget that's within their means, but as the process moves along, it can begin to get out of hand.

If you've purchased a new car recently, you know what I mean. Say for example, you want to get a nice car and you decide your budget is $30,000. Once on the lot, you see the base price on a model you like is $34,000. *Well, it's only a few thousand more, you think.* But then you start noticing some of the options. You really like the upgraded 10-disc CD changer (only another $1,000), and it's just $19.80 a month more on your monthly payment. Of course, then you see other cool things like the GPS Navigation System, the backup camera, and the Premier Audio System— so you add another $6,000. You also decide to upgrade from the standard leather package to the heated and cooled, comfort leather seats. That adds $2,160, but it's so incredible! Then you discover the Satellite Radio System, and add $486. Finally, you decide to add a sunroof, custom paint, and upgraded tires...

You get the picture.

In a matter of minutes, your $34,000 car became a $45,000 car. And remember, you started out looking for a car that would cost $30,000.

That's what it's like for some homeowners who design and build a home. Construction hasn't even started and already they've added options and selections to their home beyond the original plan. Sometimes people stretch and stretch financially to build their new home and by the time construction begins, they're under so much stress that when we have an opportunity to add a nice feature to their home (something as simple as additional crown molding), they are completely stressed out because of a few hundred dollar decision. That's often because they didn't discipline themselves to stick to a reasonable budget.

Please don't build a dream home you will have to sell before you even move in because you can't afford it.

Be sure you have a builder who will help guide you through this process with honesty and professionalism. If I notice that costs are beginning to exceed the homeowner's budget, I tell them that it's my responsibility to communicate this to them. The final choice is up to the homeowner. Ultimately, I want them to be happy *and* financially healthy with their finished dream home.

BOTTOM LINE

Build within your means so your dream home doesn't become a financial nightmare.

The Hidden Pot of Gold in Your Pocket

—⟡—

When I work with people on a building project, sometimes couples come to me with a maximum budget. They plan a budget for the lot, the home, and architecture—a complete package. When I review it with them, I spend a considerable amount of time listening, asking questions, and working to meet their particular budget. I want to make sure we maximize their investment.

Many times, however, I'd work fervently to create a design, size, and features to meet the homeowners needs and wants within the budget they presented, only to find out later that they had a hidden "pot of gold" in their pocket; they had more to spend than they let on originally.

That approach has always seemed counterproductive to me. After spending countless hours working to meet their budget, and *then* learning the couple actually has an additional amount to spend, we essentially have to go back to the drawing board to start the design process all over again. Not only is it frustrating, it also sets the construction schedule back. So if they thought they'd be in their new home by Thanksgiving, it would now be closer to Valentine's Day. After this hidden amount situation happened to me several times, I started telling my homeowners this true story:

When I first got out of college, I was ready to purchase my first vehicle. I went to the car lot and told the car salesman I wanted to spend no more than $10,000 for a vehicle. He said, "Great. Come out to the lot and I'll show you what I have."

I followed him out, and when he showed me the first car, he said, "Now here's one for $11,500." I looked at him in complete disbelief. I thought, did you not hear me? My budget is $10,000. I was thinking he'd start me somewhere in the $8,000 or $8,500 range, so that by the time I paid for tax, title, car handling fee, and other options, I'd end up at my budget of $10,000.

Admittedly, I was young and naïve and didn't know about slick salesmen. I did end up buying a car from him because I didn't know any better, but it gave me a bad taste in my mouth. I told myself then that if I ever had the opportunity to sell someone a product or a service, I'd never sell that way.

I tell homeowners this story because I finally realized they may think I'm like a slick car salesman. So I tell them I treat their money like it's my own. I will honor and take seriously the budget they give me. That's why I need the budget to be accurate, with no mysterious "pot of gold" showing up later.

If you trust your builder, give him your real budget at the beginning of the process. If you don't trust your builder, then you shouldn't be working with him anyway.

BOTTOM LINE

Hire a respected builder; then trust him with your real budget.

Choices, Choices, Choices!
Choose Before You Lose

———

I strongly recommend making most of your selections before construction begins on your home—color, cabinets, plumbing, hardware, paint, and more.

Yes—all selections!

Before I learned how important this was, I noticed that homeowners often seemed unable to make selection decisions in a timely manner. Indecision messes up the deadlines, stalls the project, and can greatly frustrate both builder and homeowner.

Randy is a good example. I gave Randy deadlines for his selections and every single deadline was missed. When it was time to make his paint selection, he asked me, "Well, when do you need it?" I said I needed it two weeks ago, and he said, "But when do you absolutely, really have to have it?" I told him "Friday" and he promised me he would have the paint selected by Friday.

Well, Friday came and went with no paint selection. I called Randy on Monday, and he told me he had an emergency, which prevented him from making his paint selection, but he would have it to me by Wednesday.

At about 4:00 p.m. on Wednesday, Randy showed up and began to put samples on the wall only to find out he needed more samples to compare to his original samples. The next day more paint samples went up. Another Friday passed and Randy said he was having a difficult time making a decision.

In the meantime, we had already completed the drywall and work on the home was at a standstill. The process had lost momentum. I was frustrated, Randy was frustrated, Randy's wife was frustrated, and the painter was frustrated. Even the cabinet man was frustrated because now his schedule was delayed.

Everyone was frustrated and all the work had stopped.

The painter wasn't sure he wanted to sign up for my next job, and my reputation as a builder started to get a little shaky.

If you've ever built a home, you know it can be very frustrating and time consuming without the help of an interior designer. You take your paint color chip along with your carpet sample and drive across town trying to match your tile with a designer deco piece for your shower. Then you take those samples to the granite supply yard, drive back across town to a cabinet supply house, and swing over to the lighting store. Along the way you're bombarded with a plethora of opinions from all of the people working at all of those stores. It's not only confusing—it's exhausting!

If your builder does not have an in-house design team to help you in your selection process, then at least retain a competent interior designer who complements your style and, as difficult as it may be to make your selections before you begin your home, do it—for your benefit, your spouse's benefit, your family's benefit, and for the benefit of the builder's and your relationship.

If you do this before the construction begins, the only thing you'll need to select after that is your toothbrush. You'll be able to enjoy the building process, and your builder can build your new home more effectively.

BOTTOM LINE

For a more enjoyable (not to mention saner) building experience, make all your selections before construction begins.

The Step Most New Homeowners Fail to Take

—⟶—

Obtaining feedback from previous homeowners is critical to selecting the right builder for your new home or remodeling project. It's a good idea for you to call a builder's previous homeowners to ask how he performed with their project. It's important to ask what the builder did very well and what some of his weaknesses were.

Of course, it's important to realize that one builder can't be all things to all people. Each builder will have some strong points, but they will also have some limitations as well. If you are looking for the "perfect" builder, I've got some bad news for you. One doesn't exist. When you look for a builder who's committed to excellence and integrity, and builds quality, custom homes, then such builders do exist.

Every builder has a unique background and unique strengths and limitations. Look for the things that matter: experience, excellence, integrity. Quality custom home builders know their own strengths and limitations. They don't shy away from them, but they work through them and provide excellent service and an excellent home—though not a "perfect" one. Here are a few questions to ask a builder's previous homeowners:

→ Did your builder finish your home on time? If not, why not?

→ Did your home come in on budget?

→ Was there ever a time you felt your builder was being untruthful?

→ Did your builder communicate to you clearly if there were any additional charges that you would incur?

→ What are your builder's best qualities?

→ What are some of your builder's weaknesses and limitations?

→ And the most important question: Would you have your builder build for you again the next time?

BOTTOM LINE

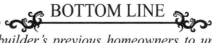

Talk to the builder's previous homeowners to understand his strengths and limitations. Also, remember that no builder is perfect.

Will I Go Over Budget?

—⟿—

If you're like most people, yes, you will probably go over your budget. On the way home from work, I occasionally stop at the grocery store just to pick up a couple of quick items. As I get out of the car, I'm thinking I'll be in and out in five minutes.

Twenty minutes later, I'm standing in the checkout line, my arms filled with items I never intended to buy. The watermelon was on sale, the blueberries were a two-for-one special, there's a new brand of chips that looks delicious, and on it goes.

Now with my arms and fingers filled with items, I'm wondering what I came here for in the first place. Oh yes, a gallon of milk and bananas! I have to set the items down and run back to the dairy department because I forgot the milk! Does any of this sound familiar? Most likely you've been there before. The same thing can happen with the new homebuilding process if you're not careful.

As you shop for the latest and greatest appliances, you may find it enticing to upgrade. After all, it's only another $840. And the carpet is only $2.00 more per square yard than your budget planned. Then you decide that you really need nicer plumbing fixtures, upgraded light fixtures, and so on. I've found that it doesn't matter how high the budget is we help establish for our homeowners. If you're not careful, you will quickly exceed your budget. If you have an appropriate electrical fixture allowance of $10,000, for example, and I increase it to $20,000, it's still easy to overspend.

Here's what I know: Even if we bumped up every budget by 30 percent, most people would spend more than their budget allowed.

BOTTOM LINE

Hire the right builder, establish a realistic workable budget, and then determine if you are, or are not, going to stay within budget.

Don't Buy That Lot!
Call Your Builder First

—⚬⚬⚬—

People sometimes call me when they are "almost" ready to talk to a builder. They've been looking at lots and have narrowed their choice down to two or three options. As soon as they purchase their land, they want to talk with the builder to discuss the home they want to build on it.

Instead of buying a lot first, we advise people to first talk to a builder. Request a meeting with your builder to look at the lots *before* you buy one. If you've never purchased a lot (and most people haven't), you could be walking into serious issues that you're unprepared to handle. Before you buy a lot, there are several things to consider. If you purchase land based primarily on price, you may discover unexpected additional costs and issues later on.

Here are just a few items you need to know:

๑ Fill dirt may be needed that may cost thousands of dollars.

๑ Often it's necessary (especially on lakefront lots) to do soil testing to ensure that the soils are suitable to hold the home in place.

๑ Testing for the suitability of a septic system (if applicable) may need to be conducted. Often, local health departments will increase their requirements for septic systems. Sometimes they require a mounded septic system and that can be an unexpected additional cost. The homeowners may look at the lots adjacent to theirs and assume that the septic system can be placed below ground, only to find that a raised mound system is now required by the local municipality, and that can be very unsightly in the front yard.

๑ Local zoning requirements may have restrictions regarding the front, side, and rear setbacks that may be more limiting than a buyer realizes.

๑ Some municipalities have lot area coverage ratios. That means restrictions are placed on how large a home you can build on the lot. In some cases, there may be existing proposals to restrict lot coverage ratios. If you unknowingly have outdated information, you may be designing a home that is too large for your particular lot. You can spend six to twelve months designing a home, only to discover that local municipality restrictions preclude the building of the home you just designed, and that may mean thousands of dollars of expenses and many months of wasted effort.

Of course, this is just a short list of issues to consider before you buy a lot. I suggest you meet with an experienced, professional builder before you sign on the dotted line to purchase your lot. Obtaining current, accurate information allows you to make an informed buying decision.

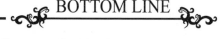

BOTTOM LINE

Talk to your builder first; buy the lot second.

How Many Bids Should I Get For My New Home?

—ево—

Recently I met with Ross at a lot where he was considering building a new home. About 25 minutes into the meeting, I noticed he was distracted by a car that had pulled up to the property.

I asked Ross, "Are you expecting someone?" He told me he was meeting with six builders that day and requesting bids from all of them. As I wrapped up the final few minutes of our meeting, Ross asked if I could give him a bid on his new home. The plans weren't complete; there were a lot of items that needed to be corrected (the specifications, including the finishes, tile, cabinetry, countertops, etc., weren't even defined), but he still wanted a bid from me.

I followed up with a letter to Ross affirming that I thought it was a good idea for him to *interview* six builders, but from my experience getting six bids was counterproductive. When all the bids came back, there would be no common basis for him to compare what was or was not included in the bids. In other words, he would be comparing apples to oranges to potatoes to carrots to tomatoes, and this would only add to the confusion of an already involved process. I suggested that Ross narrow his scope down to one or two builders that he connected with and felt he could trust, like, and respect, and put focused energy in working through the details of his new home.

A few days later at a local builders' meeting, I ran into Steve, the builder who had arrived after me at Ross's lot that day. I asked Steve about his meeting with Ross, and he said the project was too crowded for him. Ross had also asked Steve for a bid, and Steve was going to pass.

I'm not advocating you only interview one or two builders, but I am suggesting you narrow your search down to one or two builders. When I know there are many builders competing for the same job (especially if the job doesn't have a clear, defined focus), I decide to put my limited time and energy where I can be most effective. That's with people who have narrowed their scope, have a reasonably good idea of what they want, and who value what I value. Then we can put more concentrated effort into addressing their needs and concerns.

Quality custom-home builders often don't have to bid their jobs against other builders because from the onset they have made a connection with the homeowner, discussed their fee structure, and demonstrated their competency. As a result, they can give their homeowners focused service. This is important because it takes a tremendous amount of time, energy, and focus to execute the process of homebuilding with excellence.

BOTTOM LINE

Interview builders first and select your builder based on trust and respect, not necessarily on the lowest bid.

Excellence or Perfection?

—❦—

A prospective homeowner once asked me, "Will my new home be perfect?" I told him there are two kinds of perfectionists: one who asks for perfection but realizes life is not perfect, and one who is very pleased 95 to 98 percent of the time. The other type expects perfection and is never happy, no matter how well a job is done.

If you are the latter, *you must adjust your expectations before building a custom home.* Life is too short and too wonderful to take two years—or more—out of your life only to be disappointed in people and processes that are not perfect.

People build custom homes. *People* are not perfect.

It doesn't mean you can't or shouldn't expect *excellence.*

Here are a few ways that excellence differs from perfection:

❧ Excellence is taking people and materials that are imperfect and executing a process to its very highest level.

❧ Excellence is a home that's done on time. Excellence is what happens when something goes wrong and it's quickly recognized and corrected. (Trust me, when you build a custom home, things will go wrong.)

❧ Excellence is when your builder acknowledges his mistake and promptly corrects it without pointing fingers.

❧ Excellence is clear communication.

❧ Excellence is a quality home built with straight walls, functioning doors, and overall good quality.

❧ Excellence is moving into your home and having your dishwasher, garbage disposal, and gas grill all operational on move-in day.

❧ Excellence is a phone call from your builder if something unexpected comes up and the schedule needs to be modified.

❧ Excellence is having a homeowner so pleased that when the topic of homebuilding comes up he says, "Let me tell you about my builder."

Planning, designing, and building a new custom home for you and your family can be an exciting, rewarding experience if you select a competent builder who is committed to *excellence* and you have a clear understanding of each other's expectations. Homebuilding can be a miserable experience if you are a perfectionist who is unhappy even if your builder builds to excellent standards.

When Ann and I began planning and building her family's home, naturally we discussed the difference between perfection and excellence. I knew Ann understood when she told me, "Bob, the only perfect home is in heaven."

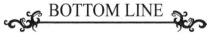

BOTTOM LINE

If you require perfection, you may need to adjust your expectations before building a custom home.

Why Picking the Right Builder
Is Half the Battle

—⁓—

How important is it to choose a good builder? It's #1 on the list! You will have a lot of decisions to make as you build your custom home—selecting colors and finishes, determining size and layout, and more. But no decision will impact your homebuilding experience more than the all-important decision you'll make right at the start. You need to choose a great builder! The fact is you can't do a good deal with a bad person. No matter how hard you work, you can't make a silk purse out of a sow's ear. The same is true with your builder.

Here are the three most important qualities to look for in a builder for your custom home:

1. Trust: Building a new home is probably one of the largest investments a person will ever make. If you don't believe your builder has your best interests in mind, you're talking to the wrong builder. You want a builder who works on your behalf, not someone who is only looking out for his own interests. When you call your builder, will you get a straight answer? If something goes wrong on your job, do you trust your builder to make it right? Believe me, when you build a custom home, there will always be bumps in the road no matter which builder you select. There isn't a contract written yet that will cover every possible condition that you may encounter while building your new custom home. Ask yourself: *What is your builder's intent?* If his internal compass is pointing north (with intentions to do the right thing, even when it's difficult), you're halfway there.

2. Competence: Does your builder have the ability to see and execute your home from start to finish? Is he able to walk you through the concept and design stage to produce a home that will reflect your needs, wants, and lifestyle? Does he have the right interior design team to complement your taste and preference? Does he have the right office staff that will politely and professionally respond to your needs and questions? Does he have an on-time, competent construction team to oversee the building of your new custom home?

Does your builder have systems and procedures in place that will allow him to execute the building of your home in an excellent way? Does your builder have a reputation and history in the community that speaks well of his business?

3. Fair Price: Does your builder charge a fair price? Most people start by looking at cost first. While price is certainly important, it's not nearly as critical as trust and competence. That's why I put this quality last.

If you know your builder is charging you a fair price for his services, and if you know he is trustworthy and competent, *look no further*. You have found your builder. Hire him and begin to focus on how to make your dream home a reality.

BOTTOM LINE

Look for trust, competence, and fair pricing in selecting a builder to build your custom home.

What About Storage?

─❧─

If you are like most Americans, you accumulate stuff. Stuff takes up space, sometimes a lot of space. Over the years, you may have accumulated things with sentimental value, seasonal items (decorations you use once a year), or extra playthings for those wonderful visits from the grandchildren.

In the homebuilding process, many people fail to take into account their need for storage, and if they do, they generally underestimate the amount of storage space they will need. In a new home design, people are generally willing to pay more for a home with adequate storage than a home with more finished space that's seldom used (e.g., extra bedrooms). Adding storage space can be accomplished in the early design stages if your builder knows this is a priority for you. The additional cost is minimal as long as your builder knows well ahead of time so he can direct the designer accordingly.

As you live in the north, you know that most homes are built with basements, which are an excellent place for storage. Some people want a separate structure, and storage sheds can be planned if requested. Another common storage solution is to create spacious walk-in storage closets within the home itself.

It's easy to create storage space in a walk-in, easily accessible, partially finished attic. Access is often located on the second story with entry from a common area such as a game room or shared space.

You should consider our country's demographics of an aging population, and be sensitive to the safety of using a pull-down ladder to access attic space. Upgrading these access ladders to light commercial aluminum ladders is money well spent for the safety and ease of access for you and for any future homeowners.

You can also design attic spaces above garages that have their own separate set of stairs. The stairs are much safer than pull-down ladders; they are often not carpeted and have a very simple handrail for safety. This is an additional, value-added benefit not only for the homeowners' safety but also for resale value.

It's important to think through your storage needs as you begin to design your new custom home.

BOTTOM LINE

Don't forget about storage. Tell your builder how much of a priority storage is to you and look for opportunities to create inexpensive storage space.

How Do You Avoid a Builder Scam?

—⁓—

We hear of new scams all the time. You can hardly pick up a newspaper these days without reading about some unscrupulous people devising a new scam to take advantage of unsuspecting people. While this may be true, it doesn't mean *you* have to become a victim. Knowing what signs to watch for can help keep you out of trouble.

Pay attention to these warning signs:

๛ **Too Good To Be True:** When a builder gives you a price that sounds too good to be true, be wary. If a builder says yes to all of your questions, walk away. If you ask him if something is included in his price, and he *always* answers yes, be cautious. It can't *all* be included! If it sounds too good to be true, it probably is.

๛ **Too Few References:** If a builder is only willing to give you two or three references, you should wonder why. Any builder can give you a few references, although it may be his brother, cousin, and very best friend. Make sure the references you get are recent and credible.

๛ **Rush to Contract:** If a builder is trying to get you to rush to sign a contract with him, you should see red flags waving and a caution light going off. Building a custom home is a big decision, and if you're rushed into signing something, you could be in for some big surprises later.

๛ **Check Online Resources:** There are online resources available where you can verify some important information on the builder. In some states, you can do online verification of a builder's credentials and license, verify how long he has been in business, the tax ID number, search for liens, find out if their workers compensation insurance is current or has ever been cancelled. Another good resource is your local Better Business Bureau.

Vague Specifications: If the specifications are vague (type of material, quality, and finishes for your home), and/or incomplete, ask that they be made specific. Vague specifications leave a lot of room for interpretation and are one way a scammer can argue later. If you sense your builder is being vague or giving you specifications that are incomplete, consider getting a bid from another reputable builder to compare the specifications from each builder. This will help you raise your level of confidence in the builder you choose that he is being honest and forthright about who he is and what he isn't providing in his proposal for your new home.

Insufficient Allowances: One of the most common ways that a builder could present a price that is too good to be true is to knowingly or unknowingly include allowances that are insufficient to complete your home as you expect it. The allowances provided should mean something to you. You should have a good sense as to what your allowances will buy. In researching your allowances, if you find that the level of quality that the allowances provide are consistently less than what you and your builder discussed, be wary.

A little healthy skepticism is a good thing. Respect and trust are earned and you want your builder to earn your respect. If you have any suspicions at all that a builder is trying to scam you, do not sign a contract with him, even if it means you have to start all over again with another builder. When it comes to building or remodeling your home, trust is everything.

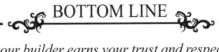

BOTTOM LINE

Make sure your builder earns your trust and respect before you sign a contract.

Financial Smarts - Part 1
Where Do I Start?

—❧—

When it comes to paying for your custom built home or remodeling project, do you know where to find your financing? Many don't. Should you peruse the Sunday papers looking for the best deal or stop by your neighborhood bank to see their rates? Do you need a mortgage lender or a mortgage broker? When it comes to finding the right home financing plan, it's really all about dollars and sense.

First, let's define the difference between a mortgage lender and a mortgage broker. Most mortgage lenders can be found at a banking institution. Their services are provided as a bank service. A mortgage broker, on the other hand, charges fees to go out and find a lender for you based on your specific financial qualifications. As a custom homebuyer, you should look for a loan officer who has experience in construction financing with the education and experience to match the banking institution. The best and most reputable lenders won't be found by scouring the Sunday papers to find the lowest rate. If you're seeking competitive rates among several lenders, don't just focus on the price. While one lender may offer a terrific rate, you may be sacrificing speed, service, or their ability to actually help you acquire a loan.

The best place to start is to ask your builder who he uses. Like his vendors and subcontractors, he should be working with a reputable competent loan officer. You may want to ask your friends for referrals as well. As the nature of markets are volatile, it's wise to have a trustworthy loan officer with sufficient experience to guide you down the path of one of the biggest financial decisions of your life. A good question to ask up front is whether the loan officer will be working with you during the entire process or will you get passed off to another person in another department.

Once you've narrowed your choice, you'll want to meet with your loan officer to determine what size loan you qualify for to build your custom home. You'll need to fill out a loan application that will focus on three key areas: your credit, your debt-to-income ratio, and your liquidity (assets and retirement reserves). While the application can be filled out and sent back by email or fax, it's probably better to take the time and fill out the forms in person. Block off at least an hour to do this and answer any relevant questions your loan officer may have. This is where all of your time spent organizing and filing will pay off. You'll need to bring the most recent copies of pay stubs, your W2 forms, and two previous years' tax returns.

Also bring your most recent statements of checking and savings accounts, retirement funds, IRA account information, and other assets that show your financial strength. Loan officers advise clients to disclose all of their assets on the application form to give the most flexibility in arranging loan approval.

One of the items that will determine your ability to obtain a loan is your credit score. A credit score is a number that is determined by the three major credit-reporting agencies (Experian, Equifax and TransUnion) and is based on historic and current data that determines your credit risk. These numbers are not set by the mortgage lenders or by the banks. Your credit report is your financial thumbprint: every purchase you've made, every bill you've paid (or didn't pay), and every loan you've applied for (car, mortgage, etc.) is logged on your credit report. A credit report is used to determine an individual's credit worthiness. Credit scores range from 300 to 850, and the higher your credit score, the more desirable you look to a financial institution for a loan. Keep in mind, the higher your credit score, the lower the interest rate you can probably get.

It is a good idea to check your credit report before applying for a loan to check for any inaccuracies, especially if you have a common name. Before applying, you may also want to pay down as many debts as possible to help improve your income ratios. Also, the major credit bureaus offer services that will educate you on how to increase your credit scores. They are the experts. Remember, your debt-to-income ratio and credit score are important factors when qualifying for a mortgage loan.

When you are ready to submit the completed application and supporting financial documents, *you may be required* to pay $300-$500 to process your application with the lender. Once all of your financial documentation is turned in and reviewed, the loan officer will submit the application to the underwriter for approval. It usually takes 3-5 days to hear whether you've been approved or denied for the loan. An approved loan will usually come back with a capped interest rate for a specific period of time (30, 60, or 90 days). Once you receive the call from your mortgage loan officer with the good news, you're on your way to the next step of the financial process.

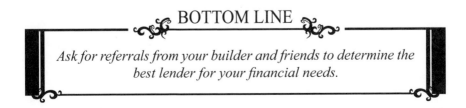

BOTTOM LINE

Ask for referrals from your builder and friends to determine the best lender for your financial needs.

Financial Smarts - Part 2
What Loan Is Right For Me?

—⚮—

O nce you've been approved to receive a new loan to build or remodel your custom home, the next step is to determine the best loan for your needs. There are a variety of loans to choose from, each with their own set of rules and terms. Your loan officer can walk you through all of the options and help you choose the right one.

While shopping for financing, you'll want to consider a "Construction-Permanent" loan. A Construction-Permanent (or Construction-Perm) loan has two phases: the construction phase and the permanent phase. The construction portion of the loan funds the construction activities during the building phase of your home. In this phase, you will make monthly payments based on how much money is drawn from the lender. As construction progresses, more money will be drawn from the loan. If you'd like to know just how much money is due and when, your mortgage lender can print out a spreadsheet detailing a fairly accurate estimate. With a Construction-Permanent loan, there is one set of closing costs that are paid at the front end.

During the construction phase, builders will typically receive a deposit when the contract is signed and then will draw from the loan during the following stages: slab pour or when the block basement is put in place, framing completion, drywall completion, cabinet completion, and the last draw will occur when the home is completely done. An independent inspector hired by the lender will come out to the construction site at each of these stages and check on the home's progress so the lender can release more money to your builder. Keep in mind, they will *not* check for quality only to see if the builder is on schedule to receive payment.

When construction is complete and a Certificate of Occupancy is issued, the loan modifies from a construction-permanent loan to a permanent loan. At this time, monies for homeowners insurance and property taxes are due into an escrow account. This usually ranges from 1.5 to 2 percent of your loan amount. Your lender will draw up the final papers that confirm the construction phase of the loan has ended and the permanent phase of the loan is beginning. The final check is made out to you and your builder for you to sign and hand over to the builder. However, you don't have to sign that check over until you are completely satisfied with your builder's work.

There are typically no additional closing fees with the permanent loan.

Another option to consider for a loan is using your builder's financing source. Some builders offer special financing packages. Be sure to ask your builder if you qualify for that option. Using a builder's financing can be just as effective as using a bank loan. Generally speaking, it's easiest and fastest to go with your builder's financing source if they are competitive in the market.

But what if you're not building a custom home? What if your builder has a home that's already done and you'd like to buy it and move in immediately? This is the most common situation for homeowners. You will need an end loan. You can still determine whether you want to have a fixed, adjustable, or interest-only rate with an end loan.

Be sure to talk with your mortgage lender about your expectations.

BOTTOM LINE

Determine the best loan for your financial needs after discussing the options with your loan officer. With so many programs and options available, choose the one that is right for you.

Financial Smarts - Part 3
Should I Get a Fixed, Adjustable, or Interest-Only Loan?

— celo—

Many new people feel confused about all the options they have when it comes to loans. Which one is best: fixed, adjustable, or interest-only? A mortgage loan officer should be able to explain the benefits of each in detail. But here's a brief overview to get you started. Let's begin by looking at the advantages and disadvantages of the three most common types of loans.

A fixed-rate loan has an unchanging rate for the life of the loan (15, 20, 30, or even 40 years). Your payments will be the same set amount every month for the length of the loan. The fixed-rate loan is the most common type of loan available on the market today. The advantage is that you always know your monthly payment amount. The total of your principal and interest payment will never change.

An adjustable-rate loan is fixed for a certain amount of time, and then the rate resets and adjusts itself based on several market indexes and interest rate caps. Sometimes the rate adjusts up, sometimes it goes down.

Most people understand this kind of loan is more risky, but there can be some benefits to choosing an adjustable mortgage loan:

1. If you plan on selling your home within 2-5 years (prior to your interest rate adjusting), this can be a good loan.

2. If you don't have much money now, but you expect your income will go up after several years—say from bonuses or commissions—and it will be easier to make higher payments then.

3. If you're only able to put a certain amount of money towards your housing budget.

4. If your financial creditworthiness doesn't allow you to qualify for a fixed-rate loan.

Lastly, an interest-only loan means you only have to pay the interest that is due each month, and are not required to pay on the principal balance for a set amount of time. For example: on a five-year interest-only loan, the amount you owe on your principal in the fifth year is, most likely, the same as when you first took out the loan.

This type of loan works well for homebuyers in three cases:

1. If you intend to pay down the principal on your own terms.

2. If you plan on moving out of your home in a short period of time.

3. If it's an appreciating real estate market. Note: the disadvantage is if you are in a depreciating market, your home may be worth less than what you owe at the end of the loan term.

The interest-only loan was designed for people who want to set their own terms and pay down the principal as they see fit. One word of caution: it takes discipline to correctly use an interest-only loan.

BOTTOM LINE

Determine the best terms for your financial needs after discussing the options with your loan officer. With so many programs and options available, choose the one that is right for you.

Financial Smarts - Part 4

How Do I Know What My Closing Costs Will Be?

—❧—

After determining the best loan program for your needs, your loan officer will draw up a one-page document that lists all of the costs associated with the loan. This document is called a Good Faith Estimate. The estimate lists all the charges you as a homebuyer will have to pay at the time of closing. Don't be surprised if some fees are slightly higher or lower when you finally come to closing. Each lending institution has slightly different charges, which is why the document you are initially given is called an *estimate*. The Good Faith Estimate is a requirement by all financial institutions as part of the Real Estate Settlement Procedures Act of 1974. If you don't receive one from your lender, be sure to *ask!*

A typical Good Faith Estimate includes all of the lender and underwriting fees as well as other charges by the state or county. Each state is different and prices vary around the country. Some lenders will waive certain fees if you ask, but some fees are locked and will not be removed.

Usually, the first line on the Good Faith Estimate is an application fee or deposit (that fee you already paid when you pre-qualified for a loan). Next are underwriting fees, which average around $500. If you choose a construction-permanent loan, there will be several charges listed for inspections. Typically the inspections cost $50-$75 each, and you'll be required to have at least 4-5 during the construction phase. That adds up to around $450. Additional fees will be added for appraisals, and typically the lender will require at least two.

Title insurance is another requirement each homebuyer will have to purchase. It protects the homebuyer to make sure no one else can come and take the property from you. The title company will run checks on the title to make sure its clear. If someone does try to claim the property, the title insurance policy protects the homeowner.

Some states require documentary or documentation stamps. Documentary stamps are simply the state charging a percentage on your mortgage note. This is one of those charges that can't be removed from the Good Faith Estimate. Another required payment to the state is intangible taxes. Intangible taxes are based on the mortgage amount. Both of these taxes have to be paid before a property is deemed legal. *These costs are a small percentage of your loan amount.*

Other miscellaneous charges include recording fees by the county to record the home's deed and mortgage note. These usually cost around $200. If you are building a custom home, some lenders will require a survey of the land before construction can begin. There may be additional fees that come after the survey, depending on the condition of the land.

This is not an exhaustive list of all the fees, but it will give you a quick snapshot of what it takes to close a loan. All of the costs on the Good Faith Estimate are one-time fees and required to be paid by the homebuyer at the closing of your loan. If you are unfamiliar with any fee, have your lender explain them to you in detail.

BOTTOM LINE

Be sure to ask for a written Good Faith Estimate from your lender outlining all of the fees associated with closing your home loan, and be certain to ask for an explanation of any items you do not understand.

What Kind of Warranty Can I Expect?

—❧—

An important question to ask your builder within the first few meetings is, "What kind of warranty can I expect?" You'll want to know if he provides the minimum warranty allowed by law or if his reputation and written warranty exceed your expectations.

Most builders provide a one-year warranty on their work. Some builders may offer a Third-Party warranty that covers your new home for up to 10 years. Be sure to ask your builder if he offers this. But what's most important is what previous homeowners say about the warranty. The warranty can be an extension of marketing. It's a good idea to call the builder's previous homeowners and ask how your builder did with the warranty and if there was anything he refused to do for them. Did he exceed expectations not only during the warranty period, but did he also show a willingness to correct things beyond the warranty period?

We can make choices to handle things that are not required, and for this reason we continue to get referrals over and over again.

When someone buys a Lexus and something goes wrong with their car one day after the warranty expires, there's a good chance the dealership will do whatever is necessary to keep the customer happy. After all, people who buy a Lexus have different expectations than people who buy a Hyundai or a Chevy.

People spend their hard-earned money with us, and we work hard to exceed their expectations. Are we perfect? No. But I believe the sign of a great company is how you handle problems. We work very hard to exceed people's expectations.

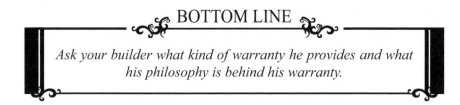

BOTTOM LINE

Ask your builder what kind of warranty he provides and what his philosophy is behind his warranty.

BOB MICHELS CONSTRUCTION

PART II

DURING
CONSTRUCTION

Don't Sweat the Small Stuff

—❦—

A few years ago, Richard Carlson wrote *Don't Sweat the Small Stuff—and It's All Small Stuff*. In his now famous book, he said, "Often we allow ourselves to get all worked up about things that, upon closer examination, aren't really that big a deal..."

That's not only good advice for life, it's especially important during the homebuilding process. I can assure you, there's going to be a lot of small stuff during the building or remodeling of your home.

Many people who frequently call their builder's office worrying about minor things make the building process much more difficult, both on the builder and on themselves. A homeowner who worries when a subcontractor is two hours late to the job, or needs to know why a two-by-four has a knothole in it, or notices some sawdust in a corner of the living room can take the wind out of anyone's sail and cause delays.

Yes, it is important to let your builder know if there are things that truly concern you because your builder wants to provide a complete and pleasurable experience. However, people who view every little thing as a "big deal" and worry about it all (especially those who call their builder daily with their current worry list) are never going to be satisfied.

Steve was someone who excelled in "sweating the small stuff" during the building of his new home. Throughout the design and contract stage of his new home, Steve was a delight and seemed to be the perfect candidate for a successful project. The trouble started when his builder mentioned the surveyors were scheduled for Thursday. Even though the survey work didn't need to get done for at least two weeks, the builder wanted to schedule it early so it wouldn't be a critical component in the building schedule.

At 7:00 Thursday morning it was raining buckets and continued to rain all day. Early Friday morning, before the builder's offices opened, Steve called because he was worried about the surveyor. The builder explained to him that because of the full day of rain the previous day, the surveyor was delayed by a day. Steve was stressed. It was the first of many times throughout the process that Steve was "sweating the small stuff."

A week later, when the material was dropped at his lot so construction could begin, the delivery truck got stuck due to all the recent rain. The builder's office got another call from Steve wanting to know all the details about why there were tire ruts in his front yard.

The day the foundation man was scheduled he was delayed because of traffic. Another phone call from Steve. Once the foundation work was prepared, Steve called to find out what day the inspection would occur. Once inspection passed, Steve wanted to know what the inspector said and why the inspection card in the permit box was signed off in black marker instead of blue ink.

After the foundation was installed, there was a bag and a half of mortar left over and two wheelbarrows of sand. Steve called to ask what was going to be done with the leftover material.

It went on and on and on throughout the entire job! Steve continued to "sweat the small stuff." No amount of meetings and explanations could convince Steve to let the builder do what he had hired him to do. It was counterproductive to the relationship and impeded the builder's ability to execute the job with excellence. The builder spent more time answering Steve's questions about the small stuff than he did looking for opportunities to build his home in the most efficient and effective way possible.

It's important to know that if you're going to sweat the small stuff (and remember, as Richard Carlson said—*it's all small stuff*), it usually will not help you get what you really want. At the end of the day, you and your builder both want the same thing: a quality, custom home completed on time and within budget. So relax and let your builder worry about the small stuff. In the end you'll be doing yourself a favor.

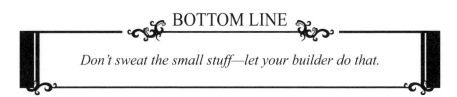

BOTTOM LINE

Don't sweat the small stuff—let your builder do that.

What Language Are You Speaking?

—❧—

"I didn't buy this home at a scratch-and-dent sale. See that chip in my bathtub? I don't want it repaired. I want the entire tub torn out."

Rick clearly was not happy. He obviously had definite expectations and, in his opinion, they weren't being met.

It's imperative to have a clear understanding of your expectations if something is scratched or damaged during the construction process. There are over 100,000 components that go into a new, custom home, and in the process of installation, something may inadvertently get scratched or damaged. I recommend you agree in writing with the builder that if he can bring the damaged item to a new, quality standard, it will be mutually acceptable. If you took delivery on a new car and it had a minor scratch, you wouldn't expect the dealer to replace the entire door or the entire car. Agree on standards with your builder before you begin.

A builder friend of mine was once hired as a mediator to help resolve a conflict between a homeowner and a builder. Instead of going to a jury trial, the builder and homeowner had agreed to binding arbitration. The mediator's opinion would be binding.

When the mediator arrived at the house, he was introduced to Dr. Jones, the homeowner, who was already dressed for work in his medical scrubs. He was then introduced to Mr. Jenkins, the builder, who arrived dressed for work in his cowboy boots, blue jeans, and a Harley Davidson T-shirt. From the start, the mediator felt they were speaking different languages.

No wonder they had conflict! They came from two different worlds. The doctor was trained in exacting measures. He was trained to do things right the first time—every time. In his world, there were no second chances. A surgeon cannot tell a patient, "Oops, I forgot. I left a scalpel inside your stomach during the operation." But the builder in cowboy boots and blue jeans was thinking, *What's the big deal? The wall was put on the wrong side of the line. We can move it in ten minutes.*

Years later (and thousands of dollars in attorney fees later) there was the angry homeowner and the frustrated builder, each one looking for something the other could not provide. The surgeon was looking for a deal, and the builder was looking for the opportunity to say he built for a doctor.

In the end, the mediator provided his written binding judgment, but neither side ended up happy. The sad thing is all of this could have been avoided if they had understood what they didn't know about the other person's point of view. I suggest you and your builder have your expectations defined and clearly written out before any construction begins. Building a new home involves so many components, and there will be things to deal with all along the way. Be clear how your builder will handle any issues.

BOTTOM LINE

Define the expectations in writing before construction begins.

Eight Common Misunderstandings Builders Have with Homeowners
... and How to Avoid Them

—❧❧—

1. *Homeowner thinks: You never finished my punch-out, walk-through list.*

At closing, the builder and homeowner assemble a walk-through list. You walk through the entire house together to determine if there are any areas or items that still need attention. It's important to have this list in writing and signed by both the homeowner and the builder. If not, the list will never end. Your builder will become frustrated when items are continually added to the list; homeowners will be frustrated because they will feel as though the builder never completed the original list. Get the list in writing and agree that if any additional items arise beyond the initial walk-through, you will create a new, separate list.

2. *Homeowner thinks: I didn't think adding two more windows to my new home would be an extra cost. After all, I'm paying a lot of money for this home.*

Changes need to be clearly communicated and put in writing to protect both parties and the relationship.

3. *Homeowner thinks: This is a shoddy builder. I never would've hired him if I had known this. Builder thinks: These homeowners have completely unrealistic expectations. I can never please them.*

Before signing a contract, both the builder and homeowner need to clearly outline their expectations. While this may take a little more time, the effort is well worth it. Pen and paper up front can solve a whole host of misunderstandings and "he said/she said" situations down the line.

4. *Builder thinks: The homeowner doesn't have sufficient funds to make changes. Homeowner thinks: The builder didn't communicate changes clearly and in a timely manner.*

Agree in writing regarding any changes that occur after the contract is signed. I also recommend homeowners pay for changes they want at the time of the change, not at the end of a job. This will keep all parties on good terms with each other and the homeowner from having any big financial surprises at the end.

5. Homeowner thinks: My builder is not taking my concerns seriously; they are falling on deaf ears.

Have regularly scheduled meetings with your builder to update the schedule, changes, homeowner concerns, and items that the builder needs in order to complete the home. That way, you don't have to feel like you are nagging the builder and he doesn't have to feel like construction is being halted every time he turns around.

6. The homeowner says he spoke to the subcontractor, and the subcontractor said he could do something for the owner without the builder's knowledge.

All communication must be communicated through the builder or Construction Manager who is running the job. This will avoid "he said/she said" misunderstandings.

7. The homeowner is speaking to everyone but the builder on matters related to the home or its construction.

Open and honest communication with the builder or Construction Manager is vital, not just with anyone who will listen. Let the builder do what you hired him to do.

8. The homeowner is continually second-guessing the builder and the decisions he is making.

Take time at the start of the project to interview and gain a high level of trust with the builder and his abilities. Also, speak to previous homeowners about their homebuilding experience with this builder.

BOTTOM LINE

Save yourself headaches by discussing all eight of these issues with your builder and resolve them in advance.

How Long Does It Take to Build a New Custom Home?

———

The amount of time it takes to build a new, custom home depends on the size, complexity, and geographic location (what part of the country you are building in).

The time it takes just to complete the architectural plans depends on how timely you make decisions and your availability to meet with your designer and builder for design meetings.

On average, developing a new set of plans that are ready for permitting can take between three and six months. Add one more month for permitting. For a home that's approximately 3,000 square feet, anticipate about an six-to-eight month construction time, provided the market isn't overly busy and there is a timely response from vendors and subcontractors. If you're building a 6,000-square-foot home, anticipate a construction time of 12 to 13 months. For a 10,000-square-foot home, add two months to the design time and another six to eight months of construction time.

These estimates assume normal market conditions, which allow for a timely response from vendors and subcontractors.

It's important to understand the realistic timeline you get from your builder and the things that may delay a timely completion process. Beware of a builder who promises an overly idealistic timeline just to get the contract. In the end, you'll be stuck with the reality timeline.

BOTTOM LINE

Ask your builder how long the design, permitting, and building process takes and what could cause delays in the process.

Should I Be Afraid of a Change Order?

———⟨⟩———

No, you shouldn't be afraid of a Change Order—*if it's done right.* What is a Change Order? Basically, it's a document that's used during the homebuilding process to let the builder know what you want to change from the original design specifications. For example, you may ask for a change because you want a different selection; you've changed your mind about countertops. Originally you wanted tile, but now you want granite. You can also use a Change Order to provide for a more functional use of space.

Your builder may also initiate a Change Order because material is no longer available, shipment delays have occurred, or a new and better product has become available.

The change listed on the Change Order must be described clearly with a fully researched price. Your signature will be required. A change may or may not affect the contract price of your home or the delivery date of the home. But, here's what really matters: You need to know! A Change Order does that.

So even if you initiate a Change Order for upgraded granite countertops and you agree to pay the extra cost, you still need to understand that shipping delays may bump the construction schedule back one to three weeks. Changes are possible, but they have consequences. The positive thing about a Change Order is everything is written down, you sign it, we sign it, and we're back in business. Nobody is going to hear "but I *thought* you said…" Changes are clear and documented.

Some homeowners may be afraid of a Change Order because most builders don't process them well. Can you imagine the chaos that would occur if we just proceeded with phoned-in instructions? You don't want to have a conversation with your builder where you both think, "but I'm *sure* he said…"

Whether the Change Order is a large or small item, it always creates a wrinkle in the construction process. Some section of work has to stop until we know if we need to change direction. We do research, make phone calls, and solicit new bids.

A Change Order may be due to a product being discontinued or there may be extensive delays in delivery of the original selection. Occasionally there are shortages of material and the builder may propose using another material in order to keep on schedule. This action would prompt a Change Order for you to review and sign. Remember, the Change Order protects you—it's *your* home and you remain in the driver's seat.

BOTTOM LINE

Minimize the number of Change Orders by hiring a builder who communicates clearly upfront, before you start building. When a Change Order occurs, make certain a paper trail follows for your protection and the protection of your relationship.

Why Do I Have to Pay a Builder's Margin on a Change Order?

—⟡—

Homebuilders and remodelers often hear, "Don't builders make enough profit so they can just include the changes as we go along? After all, we're building a custom home and we're entitled to make changes. Otherwise, we would've bought a home from a production builder."

While this seems like a valid point from a buyer's perspective, most people would be surprised to find out that builders don't make as much money as they think. We always encourage homeowners to work diligently on the front end (before construction begins) so they can keep Change Orders to a minimum. Changes can happen during the construction of a custom home, but you need to be aware of how the process works, the consequences of a change (additional time and cost), and understand the builder's margin.

Custom homes are built with as little as four changes and some with more than 200 changes. It's difficult to gauge how many changes a homeowner may make after signing the contract. Most people start out saying they love their plans and they love everything they've picked out. Yet once construction starts, we may receive nine phones calls requesting 20 changes during the first week alone!

Changes involve a lot of energy and a lot of the builder's team's time. In order to effectively process and execute changes to a custom home, a builder needs to be fairly compensated. The last thing that you want is to have your builder wincing when he looks at his mobile phone when you call. We're not saying that a builder should be able to take a trip to Hawaii because of a single Change Order fee he earns while building your home, but a fair and equitable fee that encourages your builder to work on your behalf for an excellent result is vital to the homebuilding process.

We don't encourage or discourage our homeowners to make changes. Being available to give professional counsel when questions about changes occur is our duty and responsibility. We're motivated to give our homeowners a great experience.

We once built a home for a corporate executive. John was a great client and a great guy. Our contract agreement outlined that he would provide his own refrigerator. Near the end of construction, John asked if he could use my supplier to purchase the refrigerator at my cost. Since we had a strong relationship and my focus was on serving, we allowed him to select the refrigerator. We had it delivered and only requested reimbursement of the cost of the appliance, without charging him a builder's margin.

In our original agreement, one of the items that this homeowner valued was an extended warranty, which we provided. Approximately fourteen months after John moved into his new home, the seal on the refrigerator failed and water leaked onto the hardwood floor, causing the floor to warp. When we contacted the appliance company, they indicated that the refrigerator was out of warranty and, since the home was still in warranty (because of the extended warranty period we had provided), we had an obvious problem.

Not only did we have to pay to repair their refrigerator, but we also had to pay for repairing the kitchen floor and sanding and finishing the entire floor in his home because the new finish didn't match the original finish in the rest of the home.

We learned a valuable lesson from that experience. If changes occur that deviate from the original contract agreement, then a builder's margin must be charged to compensate fairly for the time, energy, and risk associated with items that may need to be addressed at a later date.

BOTTOM LINE

Agree in advance what the builder's margin will be on Change Orders. Decide what you want before construction begins, and if a change occurs, you'll have a mechanism that provides for a win/win situation.

How to Build a Lasting Relationship With Your Builder

—❧—

W e've built and remodeled a lot of homes, and we've worked with some really great people and some very difficult people. Our most successful projects have been the result of developing strong relationships.

Here are some tips on how to have a successful construction project and make your builder love you:

𝕯► **Tell the Builder What He's Doing Right.** One particular homeowner found something good to say every time we spoke. Yes—every time. Keith didn't do this in a patronizing way; he gave me and my team genuine compliments. He looked for and commented on the positive aspects in our relationship and the services we were providing. Keith also shared his concerns with me. I would do anything for Keith and still would to this very day, more than five years after completing his home.

𝕯► **Clearly Communicate Problem Areas.** If something is bothering you about your new home construction process, clearly communicate what concerns you without anger or a condescending attitude. Give your builder an opportunity to make it right. A demonstration of a great builder is how well he handles problems.

𝕯► **Clearly Communicate Your Expectations.** Be forthright and share with your builder what you really value and tell him what is important to you. If you're clear, you'll probably get what you want.

𝕯► **Let Your Builder Do His Job.** We've been hired by homeowners in the past who seem to be agreeable, only to find out later they wanted to control the entire process and hover over us. Behavior like that makes our entire team reluctant to make a decision for them.

🔊 **Think Win/Win.** Builders are regular people just like your next door neighbors. They generally don't make as much money as people imagine, and most builders really want to do a good job. Work toward amicable solutions.

🔊 **Remember to Say "Thank You."** Builders are people too, and everyone likes to hear a thank you for a job well done.

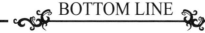

BOTTOM LINE

Follow these helpful hints and your builder will love you.

Why You Shouldn't Use Friends as Subcontractors

—ఞ—

"I have a friend (or a brother-in-law) who is willing to do the tile work in my new home for a discounted rate. I'd like to use him and save some money."

Most quality custom home builders have learned the hard way that it's not a good idea to allow homeowners to use friends or relatives for subcontracting work on the house during construction. Frequently it turns out to be a disaster for both the builder and the homeowner.

Here's one example of why: Linda wanted to use her friend's custom cabinetry shop. Linda knew the friend well and had spoken to another friend who was pleased with the cabinetry from this particular company. The builder didn't want to allow it, but also didn't want to anger his client so he agreed to let Linda use his friend's cabinet company.

The builder was promised the cabinetwork would be completed by a specified date, but the cabinets were not installed on time. In fact they were delayed several times and eventually caused a two-month delay in the construction schedule. In the end, Linda and her family moved in without any cabinet doors on the face of the cabinetry in their entire home and then waited an additional two months to have their job complete. That didn't even take into account the lost momentum or additional cost in interest carry, overhead, and other expenses as a result of the delay from the cabinet shop.

When you hire a builder, I strongly encourage you to allow your builder to do what he does best. When you visit a dentist, you expect him or her to be trained and equipped to do the job efficiently and effectively. You wouldn't think of bringing your own tools or materials, handing them to your dentist, and asking if you could save money on a filling because your neighbor or friend is in the dental supply business. You wouldn't take a steak to a restaurant and ask them to cook it for you so you could save a few dollars on the meal.

The principle is no different in homebuilding. If you use friends or your own business contacts, it will disrupt the smooth flow of work and communication of what an experienced builder does best. It could also produce conflict and put strain on your personal relationships. Trust your builder. He has vendors, subcontractors, and a labor force already in place that he works with on a regular basis.

BOTTOM LINE

Hire a competent builder to do the building; save your friends for the housewarming party.

The Top Eleven Mistakes Made by Homeowners

—cy&—

1. Purchasing a lot that is "affordable."

Solution: Remember: location, location, location. Purchase the most expensive, valuable lot you can manage, even if it means waiting on some finishes or amenities in your home. (See Chapters 6 and 25 for more on this topic.)

2. Trying to build or remodel a custom home without a professional builder. Building a custom home is more complex than most people realize. It takes skilled professionals years to learn the business and even then changes in the industry, materials, and codes make it difficult to keep up.

Solution: Find a competent builder you can trust. Negotiate a reasonable fee for his services and hire him (see chapter 4).

3. Purchasing a ready-made plan thinking it will save you money. Building someone else's design or dream (especially one that was designed for someone in another city and state) may not be the wisest choice.

Solution: Purchase a ready-made plan only if your lot is standard and you don't need to modify the plan (see chapter 12).

4. Choosing a builder or remodeler primarily because of price. The expression "you get what you pay for" applies to the homebuilding process. If you've heard horror stories about people's experience with their builder, it usually can be attributed to someone trying to get a deal.

Solution: Your home is a major investment. Make an informed, purposeful, thoughtful decision and don't be lured by the lowest bid (see chapter 17).

5. Biting off more than you can chew. In an appreciating market, the rise in value can cover this mistake, but in a flat or declining market, it can be disastrous.

Solution: Know what you can afford and stick to your budget (see chapter 24).

6. Hiring a builder or remodeler when your gut instinct tells you not to.

Solution: After careful research and comparing builders, go with your instinct, not the discounted price (see chapters 4 and 28).

7. Making choices for your home that only you love but everyone else hates.

Solution: Get good counsel from your builder, designer, interior designer, and real estate professional before you make your decisions (see chapter 14).

8. Expecting workers to be on your job every day from 7:00 a.m. until 4:00 p.m.

Solution: Recognize that some days no work is scheduled at all because inspections may be taking place or rain has caused a change in the schedule (see chapter 36).

9. Underestimating the importance of making most of your selections before construction.

Solution: Make selections prior to construction and enjoy the building process (see chapter 22).

10. Homeowners giving direction to subcontractors on the job.

Solution: Communicate only with the Construction Manager or builder. The Construction Manager is the only person on the job who has all the information related to your project. Subcontractors have only one piece of the puzzle. You can visit the job site during scheduled appointments with the Construction Manager who can answer your questions and explain what you will be seeing.

11. Not understanding the "Change Order" process.

Solution: Discuss the builder's Change Order process with him and be sure you are clear with how it works. Cooperating fully with this process will go a long way toward your enjoyment of the whole project (see chapter 40).

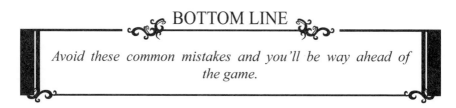

BOTTOM LINE

Avoid these common mistakes and you'll be way ahead of the game.

How to Maximize Your Valuable Investment

—�⁓—

Y ou know how you feel when you drive a new car out of the showroom? You don't want any dust, dirt, or stains to ruin the beautiful seats on the inside or paint on the outside. You keep the interior clean and regularly wash and wax the exterior to keep it spotless. A little preventative care can go a long way in preserving the life of your new car. The car manual provides a maintenance plan that highlights key times to perform routine care to keep the engine running smoothly and the rest of the car performing at its peak.

A new custom home does not typically come with a "user's manual" much like the new car. However, because it is one of the biggest investments people make during their lifetime, it's wise to take care of it from the start. A little planning and elbow grease will go a long way toward keeping your home clean, maintaining its value, and avoiding costly repairs later on. If you're not that handy around the house, you might want to consider hiring a professional to tend to things that need cleaning and maintaining. This will be money well spent.

Here is a home maintenance plan with some suggestions for maximizing enjoyment of your new home and maintaining its value:

🔖 **Clean and/or replace heat recovery ventilator, filters, and intake hoods:** 2-4 times per year or arrange to have this done for you. Your equipment will not function as designed unless you perform proper maintenance on the filters.

🔖 **Flush the Air Conditioning Condensation Line:** This preventive maintenance measure costs only pennies but has real, lasting value. Flush the air conditioning condensation line with a cup of bleach twice a year to avoid algae buildup and blockage. This simple preventive step will save you the stress of your line becoming backed up, allowing water to pour through the dry wall.

❧ **Clean the Gutters and Filters:** Have your home's gutters cleaned at least twice a year to avoid leaf buildup. Also be sure to change (or clean if they are reusable) your air conditioner's filter every three months. A clean filter helps your unit run more smoothly and saves you money on your electric bill. A clean filter also increases the life of your air conditioning unit. Nothing is more frustrating (not to mention costly) than having to install a new air conditioning unit in the middle of the summer.

❧ **Replace with Fresh Batteries:** Daylight savings time is a great reminder for this step. In the fall and spring, when you adjust your clocks, replace the batteries in your smoke alarm. As an extra note, be sure to check your irrigation clock every few months to ensure proper operation.

❧ **Avoid Abrasive Cleaners on Hardwood:** If you have hardwood floors, it's important to keep them clean in order to extend their beauty and life. However, be careful to never use wax or harsh cleaners on your hardwood floors. The chemicals could permanently damage the flooring and result in a costly fix.

❧ **Garage Door Safety Reminders:** Two important things to keep in mind if you have a garage door opener. First, never remove the garage door obstruction sensor. This safety feature is designed to prevent the overhead door from coming down on a child or animal and injuring or killing them. Check the sensor every few months to make sure it is working properly. Second, it's important to never try any type of garage door spring maintenance or adjustments by yourself. If the tightly coiled spring somehow comes off, it can cause serious injury. Always hire a trained installer or maintenance professional to assist you.

❧ **Check and Reseal:** Check the exterior of your home twice a year for any signs of expansion or contraction. Cracks may allow water to seep in causing extensive damage to the interior walls. Caulk cracks and seal wood to prevent future problems.

While this maintenance plan is not comprehensive, it does include some of the most important items every homeowner should do to protect their investment. Your home may have some additional needs to consider.

Why not take this maintenance plan and find a creative way to remind yourself to do these activities? Perhaps you could write reminders on your wall calendar, schedule them into your Day-Timer, or set up reminders that will pop up on your computer. However you decide to do it, these regular maintenance items will maximize your home's value and maintain its beauty for years to come.

BOTTOM LINE

Keep up with routine maintenance and cleaning around your house, or consider hiring professionals to protect your new investment.

What Can I Expect After I Move In?

—⌇—

Imagine it's been a few months since your home was completed. You've moved the furniture in, decorated your favorite spots with mementos and other personal belongings, and even hosted a few housewarming and dinner parties. Your home is the envy of the neighborhood and your friends marvel at the attention to detail and excellent craftsmanship. But there are no perfect homes, and a fact of new home construction involves the foundation settling and minor cracks appearing. Many of the cracks appear because your home is adjusting to temperature and humidity changes. While our company will dehumidify or add humidity as needed depending on the season during the finishing stages of the homebuilders can't build your home under factory controlled conditions. So don't panic when minor cracks appear. This is completely normal!

To help ease your fears, here's a list of common situations that occur in new homes. Builders are often asked these questions (and plenty more) from panic-stricken homeowners who fear their perfect home is now laden with problems. Remember, thousands of components were used to put together your home over an extended period of time, so settling and minor adjustments should be expected. A good builder will address your concerns promptly and work with you.

We make time and are available to answer our customers' questions about the maintenance of their homes. We can and do set our customers up with service companies to maintain their landscape, paint, electrical and HVAC systems. Be sure to ask builders you interview how they can help you maintain your home.

So what can you expect?:

🔖 **Crown Molding Cracking:** This is very common and no way around it. Expect to find minor cracking and separation in your crown molding, especially in two-story homes. Settling, heat expansion, and contraction will occur as your home acclimates to the new temperature conditions inside from running your air conditioner and heating systems. This does not mean there is anything structurally wrong with your home. Cracks in your crown molding actually look worse than they really are. A qualified handyman can caulk these minor cracks within minutes, and after the repair you shouldn't be able to tell there was ever a crack at all. A good preventative measure is to maintain your whole house's ventilators and humidifier to minimize cracking in paint.

𝄞 **Grout Cracking:** Another common spot to find minor cracking is in the tub and shower area. You may notice cracks appearing along the grout lines between tiles or in the corners of the tub or shower. Again, a handyman with the appropriate sealant can take care of this. It's a good idea, however, to add the sealant quickly to prevent moisture from seeping behind the tile and causing further damage.

𝄞 **Hardwood Expansion and Contraction:** If you have hardwood floors professionally installed in your home (not constructed from a pre-fabricated kit), you can expect to find some minor cracks appearing over time. The hardwood acclimates to the temperature of your home (again due to cool air and heat) after installation and the wood planks will expand and contract. This is normal!

𝄞 **Door Adjustments:** Even doors and door frames will need time to adjust to the temperature after a new home is finished. The doors, locks, door handles, and deadbolts may need some minor adjustment. This is completely normal.

𝄞 **Cracks in the Sidewalk, Driveway and Garage:** It is not uncommon for minor cracking to occur along concrete sidewalks, driveways, and even inside the garage. Expansion and contraction also happens here because of the varying temperature conditions that the concrete is exposed to. As long as you don't notice a difference in the height of the concrete on either side of the crack, don't worry. These cracks are normal. It does not mean that there is anything wrong with the concrete foundation. Typically cracks in concrete are not mended unless there is a height difference between the concrete on either side.

𝄞 **Receptacle Not Working:** If a receptacle (wall plug) in the bathroom, kitchen, garage, or in the home's exterior mysteriously stops working, don't be alarmed. It may just be a tripped circuit. The current electrical code requires builders to put in a receptacle called a GFI, or Ground Fault Interrupter. This measure is added for your safety to prevent accidental electrocution. These receptacles have an internal trip circuit built in that acts as a safety mechanism when there is water and electricity coming in contact. If there is an electrical surge, the receptacle will trip the GFI and automatically cuts off the electricity. Since four or five receptacles can be located on one circuit, it may be necessary to reset it. You'll need to look for a small button on the receptacle and push it. The button is usually located on the bottom or near the bottom of the receptacle site. If your receptacle continues to trip on a regular basis, call your builder or electrician to check out the problem.

This is by no means a complete list of situations that may occur after you move into your home. If you have a more specific question or situation, contact your builder to determine the best approach to fix the problem.

BOTTOM LINE

Some settling is likely to happen after you move into your home, and some cracks may appear. Don't panic. The fix is usually easy, and it doesn't mean you have a defective house.

Is Going "Green" the Way to Go?

———❦———

Today many builders and home buyers are concerned about preserving the environment. With increased attention on the condition of our planet, "green building" has become a sought after choice for homeowners.

But what does green building mean? In its simplest terms, green building is making your home more environmentally friendly. It means increasing your home's efficiency so it makes better use of things like water, energy, temperature control, and construction materials. It's about using resources effectively so you reduce the impact of your home on the environment.

While building an environmentally friendly home sounds good to most people, they usually want to know two things: what can I do and how much will it cost me? Let's address the last question first.

You may have heard that building green is more expensive. While that may be true in some instances, it doesn't have to be. In today's market some elements of green building can cost more initially, but many do not, and some even cost less. Factor in energy savings over time and the increased durability of many of the green building products, and any additional up-front cost becomes much easier to justify. Also, some mortgage companies now offer reduced mortgage rates to homes built green.

To answer the other question, let's take a look at a few things you can do to make your new home more environmentally friendly.

❧ **Indoor Air Quality:** Install a Heat Recovery Ventilator and a good quality humidifier in your home. These two components should be tied together with your HVAC components with a quality control system (such as "Honeywell's Prestige 2.0" control). Indoor air quality is very important to you and your family's health. Good ventilation and humidity control is also important to the building components, windows and the wall systems of your home.

❧ **Heating and Cooling Equipment:** One of the most important things you can do to make your home more "green" is to carefully consider your choice of heating and cooling equipment. The heating/air conditioning system should be built and installed with the highest SEER (Seasonal Energy Efficiency Ratio) rating possible. The greater the SEER rating, the more energy efficient your unit will be.

The system should also be sized appropriately to effectively cool or heat your home without being oversized. In fact, it is often better to err on the side of being undersized by half a ton than oversized. (Note: A "ton" is a unit of energy used to measure output. Typically you need about one ton of output for every 400 square feet of your home.) Many builders don't recommend that you oversize the tonnage of your home's AC system. The most efficient homes often run on a system designed to be 10 percent smaller than typical installations. A good air system should also be installed with as few bends and connections in the ductwork as possible to minimize the risk of gaps and voids.

We have installed many geothermal heating and cooling systems in our new homes and remodeling projects. They work well and depending on the cost relationship of electricity vs. fuel oil, propane or natural gas, they can be very cost effective and will pay back within 4-7 years. We have more information on these systems on our website at *www.michelshomes.com*.

❧ **Insulation:** Let's start at the bottom. The foundation and basement slabs of your home or addition should be insulated. I recommend R-15 foam for the foundation walls, and R-10 for the area below new concrete slabs. If it's within your budget, one great option is to have your home insulated with a foam product installed in the exterior walls and ceiling. When installed correctly, foam can be quite effective. On top of the good R-values (a term used to measure how well insulation resists the flow of heat or cold through it) foam can fill cracks and crevices in ways that traditional insulation can't. If a foam product can't be used, great care should be exercised to make sure the installation is done to eliminate as many gaps and penetrations as possible. My company has recommended soft foam insulation to our customers for the past twelve years.

❧ **Home Orientation:** To reduce energy loads, it's important to design and position the house in such a way as to minimize exposure to the hot sun while taking advantage of cooling breezes. Whenever possible, the front door or the house's longest wall should be set to within 5 feet of true south. It may also be important to landscape in such a way to create windbreaks for the home or create shade to increase efficiency. Good window placement can increase natural light while reducing the need for electric lighting.

➤ **Windows and Doors:** Windows help make a home beautiful, but they can also waste a lot of energy if they let in heat in the summer, cold in the winter, and drafts anytime. To get more energy-efficient windows, select ones with good insulation values. Some have special coatings that can help repel heat. Others are double- or triple-paned that helps insulation. Some energy-efficient windows have non-toxic gas between the panes such as argon or krypton that provide better insulation than air. Even the window frames can affect how efficient they are. For example, aluminum frames typically provide lowest insulation level. Wood, vinyl, and fiberglass are better. Warm-edge spacers are even better. Certain window coverings like reflective blinds and shades can also generate incredible savings on energy usage. When it comes to doors, make sure they have a tight fit and use excellent weather stripping. Some new door frames include a magnetic strip that creates a tighter seal and reduces the amount of air that leaks out. Some of the best core materials for a door include fiberglass and foam. If a door has glass, it will be more energy efficient if double or triple-paned insulating glass is used. Buy the best windows available that you can afford. Consider using triple pane argon filled glass, especially on North and West facing windows.

➤ **Roofing and Exterior Paint:** Consider using reflective roofing and lighter exterior paint colors. These two items offer a cooler home by reflecting the sun's rays rather than absorbing them. Roof choices (reflective) and lighter paint colors can create double digit drops in exterior surface temperatures, which can result in greater energy savings.

➤ **Building Materials:** Choose to use "earth-friendly" products and building materials whenever possible.

Typically, these include:
- products made with recycled content
- products that conserve natural resources
- products that avoid toxic emissions
- products that are rapidly renewable such as bamboo, cork and straw
- use lumber that is provided and/or purchased FSC/SFI/CSA certified
- locally sourced building products

- **Water Systems:** Consider installing tank less and "point-of-use" water heating systems. These systems do away with the traditional standing hot water tanks and more efficiently heat water for the home. They are also more cost effective.

- **Appliances:** Consider installing "Energy Star" rated appliances. Energy Star is a program backed by the government that identifies products with high energy efficiency. These products often last longer and are more economical to operate than non-Energy Star rated appliances.

- **Recycling:** We recycle our waste products generated during construction. We also repurpose reusable products during remodeling. Usable appliances, windows, plumbing fixtures, beams are given away on Craigslist in the "Free stuff" category. It goes fast!

- **Durability:** Choose high quality and durable products for your home. If you end up tearing out a component or exterior product in 5-10 years because it did not perform well, that product ends up in a landfill, and you spend additional money to replace it. Save your pocketbook and the environment by using proven durable building products.

BOTTOM LINE

Building an environmentally friendly home cannot only save you money over time, but also helps save the environment. But keep in mind, incorporating green features into your home early is critical to its success.

PART III

HELPFUL CHECKLISTS

This book would not be complete without a "Helpful Checklists" section. Each checklist is designed to make it easy for you to keep on track throughout the entire homebuilding process. You may want to review the lists and check off the items as you go through each phase. It can be helpful to take them with you to meetings with your builder or to the building site.

Your builder may have his own checklists for various stages of the design and build process. While they may differ in some details, they will most likely be quite similar.

These checklists have been helpful and valuable to our homeowners and to our company. They allow us to verify items that are significant in the design and construction process and make the process more efficient.

The following checklists are not exhaustive; they simply highlight some of the "must do's" while your new home is being built. We hope these tools will help you in your homebuilding experience.

Check List #1
What to Do Before You Hire a Builder

—⚬ঞ৹—

⚬ঞ৹

- ☐ 1. Look at some of the builder's homes currently under construction.
- ☐ 2. Look at some of the builder's completed homes, with or without the owners present—your choice.
- ☐ 3. Have the builder provide a list of previous homeowners.
- ☐ 4. Call two or three previous homeowners this builder has worked for and ask them key questions (see Checklist #3).
- ☐ 5. Become comfortable with the contract documents before signing.
- ☐ 6. Decide on your homebuilding budget.

Check List #2
Top Questions to Ask a Potential Builder

—⟡—

☐ 1. Why should I hire you?

☐ 2. What is your fee structure?

☐ 3. How do your fees compare to other builders' fees?

☐ 4. What are your weaknesses?

☐ 5. What makes you different from other builders in this market?

☐ 6. What type of warranty do you provide, and what is your philosophy on warranty?

☐ 7. What was your worst building experience with a homeowner, and what did you learn from it?

☐ 8. How long have you been building?

☐ 9. What is your education?

☐ 10. How many custom homes have you built?

☐ 11. How many homes will you have under construction at the time my home will be built?

☐ 12. How many homes do you build per year?

☐ 13. How do you handle changes?

☐ 14. How many Change Orders would you consider average in building a home?

☐ 15. Do you supervise the building yourself, or do you have a site supervisor?

☐ 16. Can I meet the person who will be running my job?

☐ 17. How often do you come to the job?

☐ 18. What work do you do with your own crews, and what work do you subcontract out?

☐ 19. Do you have contracts with your subcontractors? Can I see a sample?

☐ 20. Can you provide us with a bank reference?

☐ 21. Can you provide us with a copy of your insurance certificate?

Check List #3
Top Questions to Ask Your Builder's
Previous Homeowners

—⟨�‿⟩—

—⟨∿⟩—————————————————————————————

☐ 1. Why did you select this builder?

☐ 2. Did your builder demonstrate character and integrity during the time you knew him?

☐ 3. Did you feel your builder had your best interests in mind?

☐ 4. How well did your builder communicate Change Orders to you?

☐ 5. Did your builder treat you in a respectful, honorable way, and did he communicate clearly with you?

☐ 6. What was the worst thing that happened during your building process?

☐ 7. What would you do differently if you had to build your home all over again?

☐ 8. Was your home built on time?

☐ 9. Was your home completed on budget?

☐ 10. Was there ever a time you felt your builder was being untruthful?

☐ 11. Did your builder exceed your expectations?

☐ 12. What were your builder's best qualities?

☐ 13. What were some of your builder's limitations and weaknesses?

☐ 14. Would you use this builder again? (The most important question of all!)

————————————————————————————— ⟨∿⟩—

Check List #4
Before You Begin Construction

—ᘓᗖ᠈—

Review the following items with your builder at the job site before construction begins. This is not intended to be an exhaustive list; it includes the main things to check before you begin. Ask your builder to explain any items not clear to you.

—ᘓᗖ᠈————————————————————

☐ 1. Verify with your builder the height of the finished floor and all porches.

☐ 2. Verify with your builder the type of material used on all porches.

☐ 3. Verify with your builder all floor outlet locations.

☐ 4. Verify with your builder any slab/recessed areas for hardwood application.

☐ 5. Verify with your builder all hose bib locations.

☐ 6. Verify with your builder electrical meter locations.

☐ 7. Verify with your builder layout and location of driveway and sidewalks.

☐ 8. Verify with your builder well and septic locations (if applicable).

☐ 9. Verify with your builder pool equipment location (if applicable).

☐ 10. Verify air conditioning locations. Is the unit too close to the master bedroom window?

☐ 11. Verify that lot drainage conditions are correct.

————————————————————ᘓᗖ᠈

Check List #5
Before Your Builder Hangs Drywall

—❧—

R eview the following conditions at the job site with your builder prior to hanging drywall:

❧

- ☐ 1. Spot check room dimensions with your builder.
- ☐ 2. Review all door swings with your builder with electrical switch placement in mind.
- ☐ 3. Verify with your builder location and quantity of all electrical outlets, switches, cable TV, computer, speaker wires, etc.
- ☐ 4. Verify any additional electrical outlet needs with your builder such as sockets, switch lights or holiday lights, receptacles, or convenient overnight mobile phone charging locations.
- ☐ 5. Review with your builder placement of master shower valves for easy reach to avoid scalding.
- ☐ 6. Verify cabinet layout and sink locations with your builder.

Check List #6
3 Weeks Prior to Closing

—ളৡ—

☐ 1. Call your insurance agent to put homeowner's insurance in effect. (If there are current hurricanes, it can affect the ability to put insurance in place.)

☐ 2. Call your builder to verify the tentative walk-through date.

☐ 3. Call electric company to schedule service in your name.

☐ 4. Call telephone company to activate telephone service.

☐ 5. Call cable company for TV hook-up.

☐ 6. Call water municipality to schedule water in your name.

☐ 7. Call gas company to schedule gas service in your name.

☐ 8. Call pool service company for pool cleaning contract.

☐ 9. Call lawn service company to put contract in place.

Check List #7
The No-Sweat List for Closing and Final Walk-Through

—❧—

This checklist will guide you through the process of what will happen on that long-awaited day—your closing day! After many months, it is finally time to hand you the keys. One of the important closing day events will be for your builder to walk through the entire home with you. This is an opportunity for the builder to instruct you about certain aspects of your new home and to point out locations with critical information.

A good builder will have his own checklist, but this list will let you know what to expect, and you can check off your own items as you walk through your beautiful, new, custom home together. It's also a great time to ask any questions.

❧

☐ 1. Verify that keys work in every lock throughout the entire home.

☐ 2. Obtain garage door openers.

☐ 3. Obtain all extended warranties.

☐ 4. Obtain owner's manuals for all appliances.

☐ 5. Run the dishwasher through a cycle to be sure it works and there are no leaks or other problems.

☐ 6. Verify garbage disposal operation.

☐ 7. Verify gas hook-up to all appliances.

☐ 8. Verify hot water heater and recirculating pump operation.

☐ 9. Learn location of all air conditioning filters.

☐ 10. Locate emergency water shut-off valve.

☐ 11. Obtain subcontractor emergency phone numbers and information.

☐ 12. Obtain all final waiver of lien notices.

☐ 13. Obtain the Certificate of Occupancy.

☐ 14. Obtain final survey.

☐ 15. Obtain final Change Orders calculations.

☐ 16. Obtain an updated list of all colors and finish selections.

❒ 17. Transfer utilities to occupant's name.

❒ 18. Verify gas grill is working.

❒ 19. Obtain home warranty.

❒ 20. Obtain termite certificate.

❒ 21. Schedule a two-week walk-through follow-up date with your builder.

The Savvy Homeowner's Glossary
45 Indispensable Words Every Homeowner Should Know and Understand

1. Adjustable Rate Mortgage (ARM): A mortgage interest rate that changes based on an index over time.

2. Agreement of Sale: A sale contract.

3. Amortization Schedule: A schedule showing how the monthly mortgage payment is applied to the principal, interest, and the current mortgage balance.

4. Appraisal: An evaluation of homes within the surrounding area to determine the market value of the property.

5. Appreciation: An increase in the value of property.

6. Borrower: The person or persons responsible for the loan, also called the mortgagor.

7. Cash Reserve: The cash balance a borrower has left after closing, available for the first one or two mortgage payments.

8. Certificate of Occupancy: A certificate issued by a governing agency stating that the building has been approved for occupancy.

9. Closing: Finalizing the purchase and financing documents and the disbursement of funds to all parties.

10. Closing Costs: All the costs associated with the loan and the purchase, not including the actual cost of the property.

11. Commitment Letter: Formal notification from a lender stating the terms of the loan.

12. Contingency: A specific condition to an agreement or contract.

13. Credit Report: A report of credit history used to determine an individual's credit worthiness, usually provided by a credit bureau.

14. Debt-to-Income Ratio: The percentage of one's earnings used to qualify for a mortgage.

15. Earnest Money: A deposit given to a seller by a prospective buyer.

16. Easement: A right-of-way given to others to access over and across the property.

17. Equity: The difference between the market value and the outstanding mortgage balance.

18. Fixed-Rate Mortgage: A mortgage in which the rate of interest is fixed for the entire term of the loan.

19. Flood Insurance: Insurance for properties in designated flood areas by the government.

20. Hazard Insurance: Homeowner's insurance.

21. Homeowner's Warranty: Insurance that covers repairs for the home for a specified period of time.

22. Lien: A legal claim against a property that must be paid when the property is sold.

23. Loan-to-Value Ratio (LTV): The difference between the mortgage amount and the value of the property. Example: Home Value = $1,000,000; Mortgage amount = $900,000; LTV = 90%.

24. Lock-in Rate: A written guarantee by lender for a specific rate of interest.

25. Mortgage Broker: A company that matches borrowers with lenders for a fee.

26. Mortgage Insurance: Insurance that is provided by independent insurers that protects the lender in the event of a mortgage default.

27. Mortgagee: The lender.

28. Mortgagor: The borrower.

29. Origination Fee: The fee paid to a lender for processing a loan, also called points.

30. Owner Financing: When the seller of the property provides all or part of the financing.

31. Plot Plan: A map prepared by a licensed surveyor depicting the exact placement of a house on a lot.

32. Points: One-time charge by a lender. One point is one percent of the mortgage amount.

33. Prepayment Penalty: Fees charged to a borrower for paying off a loan prior to the maturity date.

34. Pre-Qualification: Pre-determining a buyer's financial borrowing power prior to a purchase. Pre-qualifying does not guarantee loan approval.

35. Principal: The total loan amount borrowed or the total unpaid balance of the loan.

36. Radon: A radioactive gas which, if found in sufficient levels, can cause health problems.

37. Refinancing: Paying off an existing loan with a new loan on the same property.

38. Settlement Sheet: The costs payable at closing to determine the seller's net proceeds from the sale and the buyer's required net payment.

39. Survey: A drawing showing the legal boundaries of the property.

40. Title: A legal document establishing the right of ownership.

41. Title Company: A company that specializes in insuring the title to the property.

42. Title Insurance: Insurance that protects the buyer and the lender against losses arising from disputes over ownership of the property.

43. Title Search: A search of legal records to ensure that the seller is the legal owner of the property and that any liens or claims against the property are identified.

44. Transfer Tax: State or local taxes due when title to property transfers from one owner to the other.

45. Underwriting: The process of evaluating a loan application to determine whether or not it's acceptable to the lender.

A Final Thought

—⎯⎯—

A t Bob Michels Construction, our company philosophy has served us well for four generations: *people are our business.* We believe that the home building and remodeling experience is more than just a business transaction; it is a long-term relationship built on trust.

Building relationships may be a tall order for some builders, but since my father drew up his first home plans, our company has made a commitment to provide an extraordinary level of personal service and attention to detail to ultimately create an enjoyable living space for our customers. I believe that the builder-customer relationship should be as strong as the foundation their home is built upon. I have many clients whom I still call my friends even years after the completion of their home. We believe we are doing something right, as 90% of our new customers come to us as referrals from our previous customers.

Each of our customer's homes are a unique expression of their vision and lifestyle. I relish the challenge of making each customer's dream home come to fruition. But I cannot meet these challenges alone. Over the years, I have built a team of craftsmen who work together and never compromise on quality. I look for experts and craftsmen who are the right fit for each individual job. It is my job to ensure that each and every component of my customer's home is made by someone who is as invested in the project as myself and the future homeowner. With the right people, the final closing will be an enjoyable experience.

I keep my late father's business card with me. On the back, it reads, **"The bitterness of poor workmanship remains long after the sweetness of low price is forgotten."** My hope is that after reading this book, you can use my father's words and mine to take confident steps toward realizing your dream home. While a good builder does not compromise on their customer's dream home, a homeowner should never compromise on their builder.

Bob Michels

About Bob Michels Construction

For four generations, Bob Michels Construction has set the standard for high-end custom homebuilding and remodeling in the Twin Cities' suburbs. Bob and his son Andy provide a unique and personal building relationship for each client.

Like his father and uncle before him, Bob Michels holds fast to the principles of integrity, quality, and value. Not only are these values a company tradition, they also make each building and remodeling project an enjoyable experience for everyone. Bob and Andy look to create enduring relationships with each customer that go beyond the final closing on their home.

Bob Michels Constructions believes in taking the lead in building trends in Minnesota. In this vein, the company builds durable and energy-efficient homes that have each unique customer's future needs in mind. The award-winning company has received accolades for its design and construction work, and was named Remodeler of the Year in 2011 by the Builders Association of the Twin Cities.

For more information on Bob Michels Construction, please visit **www.michelshomes.com.**

About the Authors
Bob Michels
Owner
Bob Michels Construction

—⸎—

Bob Michels Construction is a fourth generation custom homebuilding company based in North Oaks, Minnesota. Bob and his son Andy Michels continue their company's tradition of providing his customers with an extraordinary level of service and performance. Bob Michels Construction delivers homes of uncompromised quality by going beyond the expectations of every client. In maintaining a low volume of new home construction, Bob and Andy assure that each new home and custom remodel is a truly custom experience. True to their slogan, Bob and Andy are "on time, on budget and on the job for you."

Bob received his bachelor's degree in Business Administration from the University of Minnesota. Andy received his bachelor's degree in Business Administration with a specialty in Construction Management from the University of Wisconsin-Stout.

Bob was a board member of the Builders Association of the Twin Cities (BATC), chairman of the BATC Remodelers Committee for three years. Bob currently serves as and board member and technical director of the BATC Green Path Committee. Additionally, he is the current National Director of the National Association of Home Builders Board of Directors.

Bob and his wife, Mary, live in the Stillwater area with Andy and their two adult daughters nearby.

This is his first book.

Dave Konkol
President
Konkol Custom Homes & Remodeling, LLC

—⸎—

Dave Konkol has been creating some of the most beautiful and well designed homes in Florida for more than 20 years. He is the founder and president of Konkol Custom Homes & Remodeling, LLC, a custom home building company specializing in luxury homes. He graduated from the University of Wisconsin-Stout with a degree in Construction Management. Dave is a civic leader, sports enthusiast, and marathon runner.